YOUR CARDINAL CONNECTIONS

Heal Your Life, Emotions and Soul with the Power of Crystals

Paola Novaes Ramos, PhD

ISBN: 1539726207
ISBN 13: 9781539726203
Library of Congress Control Number: 2016917910
CreateSpace Independent Publishing Platform
North Charleston, South Carolina

Conscious silence is a powerful path to healing.

Paola Novaes Ramos

To Ronald Roseo

ACKNOWLEDGMENTS

This book is a result of the unconditional love, life energy, and strength from my husband, Ronald, who from the very beginning of our relationship has encouraged me to publish a book about the healing power of crystals to the general public.

It would also never have been possible if it were not for the unconditional love, joy, and wit of both my parents, who are the fertile soil, the nurturing water, and the loving, pure sunlight from which the strength of my life sprouts.

I also want to thank my brother and sister-in-law, partners in this love-for-life journey, for their beautiful presence and support. Thanks to all of Ronald's family for their encouragement, trust in my work, and the unfolding of my crystal research.

I am deeply grateful to all my energy and consciousness masters in Brazil: Alice Schoeder, Viviane Ribeiro, Elizabeth Carneiro, Laura Coutinho, and so many others who know who they are.

And last but not least, thanks to the people responsible for possibly the most significant turning point of my career: Dr. Janet Galipo with her wisdom, trust, and loving presence; my beautiful soul sisters Maina Campos and Kuki Alves; and Dr. John Veltheim, Esther Veltheim, and the amazing BodyTalk System.

With all my gratitude, I hope all readers enjoy this ride.

Love,

Paola

TABLE OF CONTENTS

PROLOGUE

This book is a practical tool to help heal your life, emotions, and soul by awakening Your Cardinal Connections.

As a researcher, educator, and illustrator, I have developed The Cardinal Method of Life Connection, which is an energy-healing modality based on crystals and soul healing. *Your Cardinal Connections* is a book designed to bring some of the principles and techniques I use in The Cardinal Method of Life Connection to the general public.

My areas of research have always been human nature, consciousness, and the soul. When I finished my PhD in comparative cultures, I was already researching family constellations and individual life paths in the field of energy healing parallel to my academic career.

I have been researching the power of crystals since I was about fourteen years old. The Cardinal Method of Life Connection is based not only on my knowledge about crystals, but it also integrates what I have studied in the fields of moral philosophy, consciousness, family constellations, Native American cultures, Hindu wisdom, and contemporary Western spiritual teachings, and concepts such as the inner child, the ego, and the higher self. As a certified BodyTalk practitioner, I give regular present and distant sessions at Ranova Healing Center, as well as The Cardinal Method of Life Connection sessions, and they all involve crystal healing.

I hope you like this book and suggest you hold a crystal in your hand as you read it. Doing this will not only be calming and soothing, but it will also remind you of the best aspects of yourself that can be manifested in the world. Crystals in Your Cardinal Connections remind you of that—your strength, your ability of self-healing, your inner beauty, and the love you have in your heart.

Your Cardinal Connections journey begins now.

LIFE CONNECTION

If you are reading this book, you are probably interested in leading a meaningful life—a life with purpose. That means you want to strengthen Your Cardinal Connections spiritually, emotionally, mentally, physically, and financially.

Living a connected life means you know and you live according to your truth. You deepen and expand the awareness you have of yourself and the world, connecting yourself to the endless creative potential of your inner world and to universal consciousness.

This book is about self-connection and life connection. Both self-connection and life connection come to you by being in touch with what is real and what makes your life meaningful.

The first thing that needs to happen for Your Cardinal Connections to wake up is to be receptive to your Truth. Truth creates spaces for personal growth and consciousness expansion. It is the underlying current of life, and it guides the purpose of everyone's lives too.

In our human experience, our Truth usually comes with some degree of pain because it involves emotions. In many of our societies, we have been conditioned to overvalue our rational minds and to dismiss emotions as unimportant or even useless.

We are conditioned not to deal with emotions or to mostly deal with them using logical thinking and reason, instead of feeling them in their full existence.

Since a fulfilled life and an expanded consciousness ultimately promote integration of most aspects of our being, dealing with our emotions is a huge key factor for life connection, because when consciousness expands, so does life. Even if that expansion requires us to deal with pain for the sake of gaining more awareness, it is worth it.

This means, among other things, that we have to pursue our talents and increase our love. This will bring us joy and awareness of our flaws and painful experiences.

When we observe both joy and pain, we integrate, transmute, and expand our life experiences.

This process takes commitment to personal growth, and this book will help you in that path.

The question you need to ask yourself before you continue is this: **Am I willing to investigate various aspects of myself, both joyful and painful, to pursue a happier, more meaningful life?**

If you are receptive to information that will shift and expand your perspective, guiding you to your Truth (which includes all aspects of your being), you will be connected to your most wonderful talents and feelings, your creativity, your love, your strength, and also your flaws and blockages. If this is what you want, this is going to be a great journey.

As you connect to your love, your talents, and your creative powers, you will start to manifest them in the world. You will also observe and understand your flaws and blockages. As you take responsibility for them, you will be clearing and healing in your own timing.

When you observe your negative aspects, you will not blame anyone, not even yourself. You will understand the origins and root causes of your problems. You will be strong to admit what you have chosen to do and to be, and you will observe yourself with kindness without falling into victim mode.

Do not push yourself, and be kind to your heart. Take small steps and small doses of information, and read this at your own natural pace.

If it takes longer than you thought, respect your emotional rhythms. Everyone has a different natural pace. The spirit is fast, but the soul is sensitive and calm, and some people may think the soul is slow, but in reality it is patient and wise. It knows the right amount of time each of us needs to digest information.

Respect your rhythms above all else. Remember that if you or any other person is not ready to face this kind of consciousness process, it is because it takes time. It takes getting used to new ideas, new information, and new awareness.

We all have to allow our wounds to heal before we are strong enough to face expansion.

Sometimes it takes a while for the Truth of the soul to surface and for the soul to heal. Information and crystals can help your process, but they are tools to remind you that it all starts and ends in your own consciousness and your own self. It all begins and ends with your choices, your commitment, your consciousness, and your heart.

If you keep reading this book, or if you decide to stop right now, as long as it is in alignment with what feels right for you, it is the best choice. To help you make this choice, there are three things to consider and observe if you are in one of these three states of mind:

Denial Mode

This state of consciousness occurs when you are unhappy in some or many areas of your life but you try to convince yourself that your life is great. In this state of mind, we either do not see, avoid, or dismiss the unhappy areas of our lives as unimportant or even as nonexistent. When we are in denial mode, we always tell ourselves that life is great, even if it is not.

Whether we have issues with our bodies, finances, professional life, family, relationships, friendships, spirituality, or faith, we think stagnation and a so-so state of being are actually all life has to offer.

This is a state of avoidance. We know deep inside we are not happy about something—or some *things*—but we convince ourselves that we are indeed happy or content and that a so-so life is actually good. People in denial mode usually have minor to medium intensity health symptoms like insomnia, chronic pain, general pessimism, boredom, and apathy.

If this is your case, try to observe yourself and make a list of the areas of your life that could be better. Then decide if you should keep reading this book or give it a rest for a while.

Comfort Zone Mode

In this state of consciousness, we have slight to medium awareness that life is not great, and we usually know where the uncomfortable areas and tender spots are—but we decide to leave it as it is because it would take too much effort to make structural changes.

We know something hurts and where it hurts, but just do not want to make the efforts to change. We choose our comfort zones over a great life.

Comfort zone mode is what makes us keep going despite the pain or danger of our lifestyle. In this mind-set, we usually live with the lack of a higher purpose and just carry on. Survival, safety, and predictability are the guides and keys to life. There is not a lot of expansion in any sense.

After we have reached a certain point in life, we decide what the sweet spot of comfort is and deny any change. Since change is the very essence of life, things tend to become stale and boring, but we choose this instead of allowing expansion and personal growth, blocking the unknown, not allowing life to reveal itself in its fullest potential.

If this is your case, just observe it. We all have comfort zone modes in our lives, in one way or another. It really adds up to how much energy you have to make and allow change in your life.

Victim Mode
The third stagnant mind-set is victim mode, which is when you realize there really is something wrong with your life and the only thing you do about it is complain. We blame the universe, the environment, and the circumstances and wait for a miracle to happen and bless us from above, or for nothing to happen, as we remain miserable in a vicious cycle of an unfulfilling life of complaining.

Victim mode sometimes creates physical symptoms because this mind-set needs to confirm how painful and cruel life is. This enhances the vicious cycles and perpetuates toxic states of mind.

While denial and comfort zone modes tend to dismiss the truth as unimportant, a victim mode mind-set tends to vehemently—if not violently—react to the truth as a threat. In reality, that is what the truth is anyway—a threat to avoidance, comfort zone, and victimization, because it urges you to be responsible for your life and do something about your life purpose and your own happiness.

Our perception of pleasure, when we are in victim mode, is distorted—we get pleasure from pain, suffering, and complaining, instead of from true joy and happiness.

If you feel that you're in victim mode, don't judge yourself and just allow this information to sink in. Try to become aware of how your consciousness is wired and that you can change it if you want to. This can happen slower or faster than you think. Open your mind and heart to the possibility of change and see how you react to this idea.

If you feel a little dizzy when you think about victim mode, just rest for a while. Try not to engage in judgments about yourself or other people. Just allow the awareness and consciousness to enter your mind naturally and respect the changes you may want to make.

Holding Yourself Responsible
Holding yourself responsible does not mean you have to beat yourself up when you become more mindful of the areas of your life that need improvement. Actually, doing that is just a smarter way of reaffirming victim mode, and it is far from holding yourself responsible in essence.

Observe if you are ready to commit to a journey in which you will become an independent adult with self-awareness and energy to change what needs to be adjusted in your life. If you feel you are in one of the three limiting states of mind described above, be mindful of them and allow your awareness to unfold.

Just by reading the information in this book, you will already feel emotional shifts. The stories and examples are very powerful healing tools in themselves. If they resonate with your personal story, or with someone close to you, they will bring keys to healing and expand awareness on many levels. These are all real stories, and names are fictional to preserve the privacy of those involved.

If you feel that you are ready, you may begin your journey now. Take responsibility for your own life and commit to a positive mind-set. Hold your crystal, take a deep breath, and enjoy the ride.

INTRODUCTION

This book's purpose is to introduce a joyful experience with crystals to the general public so that more people can reconnect their lives to the joy of happiness and fulfillment.

It was written to remind us that life is simple and that we tend to complicate it when we disconnect ourselves from the wisdom of our hearts and when we lose contact with nature and the natural world.

When we are in touch with the Truth of our hearts and with nature, we are much more connected to our own consciousness and awareness of everything in the world, especially ourselves. This book brings practical tools that encourage us to observe who we really are and what we have created in our paths.

The practical tools are crystals, breathing, and mindfulness without judgment as you read these pages.

As you read, you will understand some of the underlying aspects of your relationships, your family dynamics, your friendships, your professional and financial life, your spirituality, and your life mission.

This perspective is called Your Cardinal Connections, which is part of The Cardinal Method of Life Connection that I created in the past decade. I broadly explain a lot of what these methods are in my YouTube channel, which you are very welcome to watch by searching for "Paola Novaes Ramos."

At this point, you may especially want to check out the video titled "Languages of Consciousness." This video clarifies some basic principles of what this book is about. And as you keep reading, you will understand what Your Cardinal Connections are at a deeper level. As you watch, I suggest you hold a crystal in your hand to start connecting to crystal energies and to focus your awareness:

https://www.youtube.com/watch?v=B7Usd3-qNVg

Your Cardinal Connections
You are now beginning a journey to get to know and understand Your Cardinal Connections. They can be described as fundamental energies that fuel your life, and I am happy and grateful to bring them to the world and share this journey of life connection and self-discovery with you.

Once you know and understand what Your Cardinal Connections are, you will see that crystals are a powerful tool that can help you connect yourself to these energies even more. They boost the energy flow of Your Cardinal Connections. Not only do they wake up the power of love within you, but they are also instruments of nature that help awaken your natural self in truth, healing, peace, and freedom.

Let us dive into Your Cardinal Connections. *Cardinal* means "what comes from the heart"—all that is essential and comes from this place within you. It also relates to how you orient yourself in the world regarding directions (north, south, east, west, up, down, center).

Your Cardinal Connections are the areas of your life that come from your heart and orient you in your path, guiding you toward the best directions to follow. They connect your heart to the world and help you create a great life.

If the cardinal areas of your life have lost connection with your heart, you manifest your life in the world with low energy. Things are probably not going as well as they could be and have the potential to be much better.

The essence of Your Cardinal Connections is deep and simple—more than you can imagine. These areas of your life give it meaning and make you happy and healthy, and they are *your physical body, your emotions, your thoughts, your finances, your job, your family, your relationships,* and *your spirituality.*

From a dense perspective to a subtle perspective, Your Cardinal Connections are: your physical body; financial and professional life; family, friendships, and relationships; your unique self and spirituality.

You will understand this in more detail as you continue reading.

The Healing Power of Crystals, Minerals, and Stones
Crystals are wonderful tools to help you reestablish the vitality of Your Cardinal Connections. With the power of crystals, your life becomes lighter and emotionally healthier in general.

With this book you will discover how this happens, and with your growing awareness, you will engage in happier states of mind. You will feel more connected and will progressively attract more experiences of joy in your heart.

Thousands of years ago, traditional cultures all over the world used crystals to help individuals, families, and societies understand the truth behind events, solve problems, harmonize conflicts, and heal emotions. Many ancient wisdoms relate to the power of the mineral world in physical health as well.

What I can say in general about crystals is that they ground and align your mind to your Truth and connect you to your heart. Not surprisingly, your body's well-being will benefit from your happier state of mind as you connect to crystals.

Crystals are literally transformers of subtle energies because they connect us to our Truth and to the Truth of the world. Since emotions are subtle energies that are as real as our physical bodies, even if they are not tangible to our physical senses, they might shift with the power of crystals.

And what do crystals have to do with Your Cardinal Connections?

They are energy conductors that can potentially organize all areas of our lives. Most importantly, their purity realigns our distorted emotions, feelings, and thoughts. This means that with the help of crystals, Your Cardinal Connections reestablish communication with the heart.

When you connect your conscious mind to your heart while holding a crystal or wearing crystal jewelry, you allow the benign, healthy flows of a natural life to enter your world. You will experience natural states of bliss, peace, and joy, simply because that is our natural state of being.

This means that the energy of our hearts is strongly connected to nature. Crystals are a wise, silent part of nature that can help heal not only our states of stress and anxiety, but also our deepest emotions, our relationships, and our souls.

The first specific thing you need to know about crystals is that they awaken natural states of **Joy** and bliss. When you look at them, touch them, and feel them in your hands, you tune into your awareness of the Truth of your heart.

This is not superstitious thinking or magic thought. Open your heart without judgment and try it—you'll be surprised by how fast your connection with the crystal is, how fast accurate information flows, and how fast you receive clarity of something in your life.

This connection and understanding lead to mind expansion and come from your subtle senses of hearing and sight, which flow into your heart as a spontaneous a-ha moment with clarifying thoughts. If you have never heard of this before, we have physical senses *and* subtle senses of sight, hearing, touch, smell, and taste that perceive nonphysical reality, such as emotions, feelings, and thoughts.

The second specific thing you need to know about crystals is that they awaken joy and bliss inside you because they are filled with **Love**. They can be considered mineral live beings.

When you connect with crystals, you will feel your truth, your love, and your emotions surface to your awareness. Since they exist in a pure state of being, their vibrational frequency is very high and raises the vibrations of your body and mind as well.

This is why crystal energy is stronger than your dreary and distorted thoughts and emotions. Slowly and permanently, if you are open-minded, open-hearted, and release resistance with commitment, you will become a happier and more joyful person. Crystal connection will help pull you out of your misery and keep you anchored, peaceful, and connected.

If you are already fairly healthy and happy, crystals will help sustain that vibration and connection to the best paths life has to offer.

The third specific thing you need to know about crystals, which was already mentioned before, is that they bring forth the **Truth** and align you with the reality of the present moment. This is the kind of awareness that surfaces with crystals, and this type of information and awareness is very simple and straightforward. You quickly realize the Truth is what it is. Once you start tuning in to crystals more frequently, you will be surprised with how accurate, precise, and objective information will come to your awareness.

These are the three main attributes of crystals that you need to know before you start your journey. Always keep in mind that they vibrate in **Joy**, **Love**, and **Truth**, and that the vibrational frequency of crystals is stronger than depression, stagnant emotional states, wounded hearts, and painful experiences. Your heart can always heal, sometimes faster than you can imagine. Crystals can help restore your heart's wisdom and encourage the integration of your soul.

One of the greatest things about crystals regarding emotional health is that they help us release painful experiences and move on. When they reveal the Truth of an experience to your awareness, emotional healing immediately takes the lead and releases the pain from the past, connecting you to the present moment and encouraging you to move on.

In helping us understand that the past is gone and that life moves forward, our hearts are set free. We begin to expand our lives into new experiences of joy and personal growth.

To gracefully bring forth the exact amount of energy and information you need in order to revive Your Cardinal Connections, the last chapter of this book teaches you how to create a hands-on experience with crystals in two practices to enhance your awareness and help heal emotions.

Once you connect to crystals frequently, each new day will be a gift of joy and expansion in your life. You will be ready for more every day. Life becomes a flow of new benign energy and experiences, moving you toward a spiral of abundance, joy, and well-being.

This has been my experience and also the experience of many friends and clients I have had in the past decade. Crystals have helped heal my emotional life and the lives of many people I love and care for. I have seen it happen hundreds if not thousands of times, and I know you can benefit from this experience too.

If you tune into the simplicity and the beauty of life, you can have many natural, fulfilling, and abundant experiences and expand into millions of new, creative possibilities.

I hope you enjoy the ride. It's time to flow.

1

HOW CRYSTALS CAN STRENGTHEN *YOUR CARDINAL CONNECTIONS*

What do crystals have to do with connection to life and with Your Cardinal Connections, especially regarding your body, finances, emotions, relationships, and soul?

Crystals are usually seen as natural objects that bring beauty to the world as ornamental objects or jewelry.

In a metaphysical sense, they are also considered spiritual tools that access higher realms and help the world heal. Usually, however, this understanding comes with magical thought or superstitious thinking and often with fantasies and escapism from reality. Instead of connecting us to reality, superstition and magic *dis*connect us from it, and it is almost always an escape mechanism from emotional pain.

In order to make it clear that the perspective of Your Cardinal Connections is anything but superstitious, understand that the physical world is animated by energy, but not in the way magical thinking tends to see it.

There is a connection between the physical reality of the world and energetic frequencies, and the idea is that this connection brings consciousness, awareness, and vitality to deal with the truth and create a great life, instead of running away from the truth and creating excuses and illusions to deal with an unfulfilling life.

Magic thought tends to dismiss or even disqualify the physical world and escape into energetic realms as if there were no connection between the two, when the best of life in word is to manifest beautiful energies in the physical world and make it a better place to live.

This is a very important thing to understand. When we see a connection between the subtle energies and the physical world, we are engaged in metaphysical and scientific thinking and committed to creating a better life in the physical world, making it a better place to live.

When we dissociate subtle realities from the physical world and our lives or areas of our lives, are a mess; we are engaged in magic thought and escapism.

One of the ways to observe the connection between energy and the physical world is through our emotions. Our stress levels interfere in the physical body. Our uncontrolled emotions can disturb our lives.

When it comes to crystals and the relationship between subtle, invisible realities and the physical world, there is usually a lot of confusion about what they are and what they do.

This is especially because metaphysical crystal properties, if not well understood by our conscious minds, can easily mislead us into magical superstitious thinking. This disconnects us from conscious awareness and reinforces what I call *spiritual escapism mode*.

The metaphysical properties of crystals are not mysterious at all. Crystals are natural beings that encourage us to contemplate beauty. They inspire us to be silent and just enjoy the beauty of life and nature, and we can contemplate the truth of reality as it is and as we wish it would be. That contemplation connects us to the best energies of our hearts and makes our lives fun and joyful.

Rather than observing crystals as supernatural and metaphysical, I suggest we think of them as natural physical beings full of love, like plants and animals and ourselves in our natural state.

Also, when it comes to the role crystals play in the expansion of our awareness, they naturally remind us that it is possible to integrate our everyday lives with consciousness, love, peace, and joy.

This does not mean you have to be happy all the time. When the contemplation of crystals brings in a connection to your emotions, it is aligning you with the reality of what you are truly feeling, be it happy or otherwise. Your personal fulfillment comes from acknowledging all emotions and allowing them to flow instead of blocking the negative emotions and shoving them to the depths of your unconscious mind.

Crystals do not *cause* you to be happier or healthier, though. In reality, they do not cause or create anything. They allow all energies, positive and negative, to surface and be released so you can live from inspiration instead of living from painful memories, as Dr. Ihaleakala Hew Len would say. Crystals reconnect you to the joy of living, but they do not create it. They wake up what is already inside of you.

They are not magic tools or relics with special powers. There are *no special powers* in crystals—your contemplation of them encourages you to connect to *your* natural consciousness and the powers that reside within you, such as beauty, love, joy, good will, allowance, acceptance, and being conscious and aware of the truth.

Crystals also help you dismiss what does not suit you, and this means the connection with them encourages you to be authentic. If you need to say no, you feel more empowered to say no and to build healthy boundaries, acknowledging the truth instead of running away from it or being run over by someone else's priorities.

I have developed a Cardinal Method Inner Child Kit with that purpose. It is a very simple and effective tool to encourage you to be authentic and build healthy boundaries. All you need is a stone bracelet and a crystal. I explain how to use it in my video on YouTube:

https://www.youtube.com/watch?v=ARYogkhk5ps

It is also on my website, www.ranovalife.com, where you can purchase your own Cardinal Method Inner Child Kit, and it is explained in detail in the last chapter of this book as well.

Reading and hearing about these healthy boundaries we can create with the help of crystal awareness is very powerful.

Crystal connection encourages you to contemplate the Truth. It will surface and communicate itself through accurate information in the form of insights. Contemplating combines both logical and intuitive thinking simultaneously.

Start observing this process when you are in the presence of crystals. Ask yourself a question, hold a crystal or sit next to one, and wait for an answer—the information that will come to you will be accurate. It will pop up, and you will know the Truth in your heart. You will be surprised with how quickly and objectively it comes to you.

As natural tools that have a high vibrational frequency, crystals are enhancers of consciousness. They calm your conscious mind down and encourage you to tune in to your truth and your heart's desires and awareness. They also encourage you to reconnect to your own abilities of self-healing, self-acceptance, and problem solving.

Because crystals do not hold distortions of the split mind as human beings do, when you are in the presence of a crystal, your alignment is stronger than negative thoughts and depreciating emotions. That is why our lives begin to change for better when we start working with them.

The insights you will get from crystals are very powerful keys to help you in emotional healing. This immediately improves the quality of your thoughts and your overall energy so that you can take better care of your physical body, your home, your finances and professional life, your relationships, your love life, and your spiritual path.

I recommend you have one or two crystals near you in the process of reading this book. Unlike superstitious or magic thinking, crystals are very grounding. They are reminders that everything you need to expand, grow, and heal as a human being already resides inside you. Crystals are beautiful, loving, fun connections with your own awareness of the world and with your inner bliss—not a magic tool, but a reminder of the magic of life.

Integration and Emotional Healing
As mentioned before, crystals bring Joy, Love, and Truth to our lives. They align us with our higher power, our higher and spiritual selves. They acknowledge our most supreme virtues and living from an integrated self within you.

This alignment with the higher self has the power to do two things. The first is that it gives you more awareness of where the roots of your problems are. The second is that it encourages you to observe your emotional wounds and distorted aspects of yourself from a more neutral perspective, with genuine love and compassion. You integrate those wounded aspects instead of denying and excluding them, and this way of living opens the paths to emotional and soul healing.

When you connect to your higher self, you know joy. You know peace and you know love. You do not react to events with anger or sadness or worry in the intensity that you used to. Your emotions are very deep and very real, but not exaggerated. You will not be afraid to experience any emotion, and when you allow yourself to feel everything in the amount of intensity that is real, you know happiness.

Happiness

Happiness is a wonderful thing, and we all want it. It can be described as myriad integrated emotional states rather than one single specific emotion, also known as joy.

What this means is that being fully connected to all our natural emotional states is a lot healthier—and happier—than the fixed idea of having to be happy and joyful all the time. An exaggerated or fake image of happiness has become almost a cultural obligation in the Western world these days. The idea of happiness in this book is more connected with being peacefully aligned with the Truth of all emotions than by forcing yourself to be happy and faking happiness because the Truth may be painful.

A good example of this is a married woman who chooses the stability of being married to a predictable and more socially acceptable man with a nine-to-five job, instead of being single or in a relationship with a man she truly loves but that has an unorthodox lifestyle, such as a book author who travels a lot. Her conscious mind thinks she is happier in the predictable lifestyle, but her heart knows she would be a lot happier if she allowed herself to be with the man she loves and adjust to lifestyle changes.

The opposite may also be true. Another example is a woman who is a single photographer and leads a very intense lifestyle taking pictures of musicians in bars at night. She likes the artistic part of her professional life, but the lifestyle of nightlife is too intense for her. She would rather, in her heart, be married to a stable man and have a part-time job taking pictures of babies and making cupcakes.

When it comes to self-awareness and consciousness expansion, there is no right or wrong when concerning what you love and what lifestyle you want to lead. All we really need is to envision what makes us happy in terms of love and lifestyle, figure out what we can and cannot handle, and make peace with our choices without pleasing others with them. Happiness is about Your Cardinal Connections and not anyone else's.

When that awareness comes to you, you are awake and conscious and feel no need to complain. However, I have seen a lot of people fall into denial, comfort zones, or victim modes even after that awareness had surfaced, because they think the work that leads to an authentic life of love and joy is too much. It is more than they have the strength to manage.

Happiness has everything to do with your inner Truth and the conscious awareness of your heart than anything else. Allowing yourself to feel the whole spectrum of emotions that come with that truth and that connection is a true state of happiness. It is not necessarily a predictable image of happiness, but it is the Truth.

In the presence of crystals, if you keep an open mind and an allowing heart, you will feel more connected to the awareness of what your individual, authentic happiness is and where it resides.

If you want, you can even make a list as you hold a crystal of the things and people that truly make you happy. They could be in your present moment or things and people you wish were in your life. As you make your list and hold the crystal, you may be surprised to find out that your lifestyle and the people you surround yourself with are not exactly a match to your heart's truth and desires. Or the opposite may occur—you will realize that they are and be more grateful for the life you have.

Silence
Another very important, crucial characteristic of crystals is silence. Crystals encourage us not only to silence spoken words, hear more, and talk less, but also to silence the mind and become receptive to what our hearts have to say. There is a lot of communication in silence—just not the noisy kind.

As natural beings, crystals encourage silence so we can hear the natural voices of our hearts. They encourage us to quiet the conscious mind down, and our information flow becomes more accurate because it is coming from the heart and not from our conditioned conscious beliefs and noisy assumptions.

The sounds of nature are also great encouraging tools to help us tune in to silence and listen to our hearts and the nature of our true beings.

And lastly, silence is a great, powerful healer of emotions. Once you obtain awareness of how you are feeling and talk about it with a friend, it is very important to lie in restful silence for a while. It really helps us heal faster instead of chattering and sabotaging our awareness and heart connection.

Awareness
Awareness comes from a-ha moments and deep knowledge that you are connected to the Truth of the world, or to the Truth of your

heart. Usually it comes after a process of self-connection and deliberate attempts to understand the root cause of problems or issues, but it can also come as a pop-up thought in your mind and heart when you least expect it.

These a-ha moments may come after meditation, after a therapeutic session, after being out in nature and moving your body, or with the simple experience of holding a crystal and focusing your mind and heart on a problem or issue you wish to clarify or resolve.

Doing the Ho'oponopono prayer is also a great instrument to increase and expand your awareness of self and the world.

What is Ho'oponopono prayer? It is a simple and effective practice in which you repeat four sentences like a mantra:

I love you.
I am sorry.
Please, forgive me.
Thank you.

These four sentences repeated together have the power to erase painful memories from the past. When you stop living from memories, you come to zero point and start living in the present moment from inspiration. This is Dr. Ihaleakala Hew Len's perspective, and you can find more information in this video:

https://www.youtube.com/watch?v=vOgHthDfeMo

Release
Once there is awareness, the next step in a life connection process is to release the problem and allow it to dissolve. Sometimes this happens simultaneously with the a-ha moment of awareness, and sometimes it does not. Some people understand the issue fully with their

conscious minds, but their hearts are blocked and there is a lot of unconscious resistance to change.

Sometimes there is not a strong enough commitment to change, and this allow shifts to happen because many people are afraid of life-changing experiences, and they are just not ready.

Do not judge anyone or yourself if that is the case in some of the areas of your life or in the lives of some people you know. Some things take longer periods to heal than others, and everybody is different.

The person you want to become will eventually shape your life, and it is OK not to make changes immediately even when you realize you are unhappy. Sometimes there is too much at stake, and the costs of change may be too great to deal with in the present moment.

The important thing to know is that *releasing* is the final step to freedom, genuine love, and a meaningful life connection. With that information, you can make your choices, and whatever you choose will be the best for you in the present moment of your circumstances.

Choose your course of action with the wisdom of your heart. You can be sure that the presence of crystals around you and in your hand will help you choose which way to go with wisdom, truth, and love for yourself and others.

2

YOUR TRUE, CONNECTED SELF

Your natural true self is already healthy and happy.

Our painful life experiences disconnect us from this true, happy, healthy self, but if we know how to connect with our hearts again, we will be in touch with that life source and begin to release distortions.

Being truly happy and fulfilled involves many aspects of our lives that must be balanced, or at least fairly balanced. We know that there is no perfectly balanced life or perfectly balanced person in all areas of life at all times. However, it is possible to improve our lives and to have better life quality and general well-being.

General quality of life comes with fulfilling needs in areas of life that are important to us. More often than not some area needs improvement. There are infinite possibilities for expansion when you are connected to your real source of life and in alignment with a higher power (God, source, universe, life flow, or any other term you resonate with).

What are the distortions or discomforts in life we tend to experience? Some people have serious issues with their health or body appearance. Others have problems in their financial and professional lives. Others have family issues or emotional and relationship issues. Others have spiritual disconnection, and some people experience problems in two, or three, or even most of the areas described above.

It is OK if it is that way. We are all on this planet to learn from our flaws and to try to become better, healthier, happier people who experience love and freedom as much as possible.

This means that in a progressive, spiritually evolutionary perspective, the person who becomes integrated once felt disconnected from our life source in one or many areas, and the person who is in pain and difficulty today always has the potential to become integrated in the present—or a whole, integrated, fulfilled person in the future.

There should be no judgments when it comes to distorted, painful, nonenergized areas of your life. We all have our issues to deal with. And dealing with them begins with clarity about where you need improvement and which is the best way to find the improvement you need.

We will start with the denser aspects of life (your body, your home, your finances, your professional life) and move in the direction of the more subtle or intangible aspects (your family, your emotions, your brain power, and your spiritual self) to get a good idea of the big picture of your life.

This is a powerful exercise, and you will be guided in every step of the way so that you can really feel your level of awareness increase.

The first thing you need to do to engage in this process is choose a crystal to hold while you read the questions. It's simple and very effective. Holding the crystal will help you tune in to the process a lot faster than if you do not hold one.

The crystal you choose will be your companion throughout this initial journey of clarity. You may think you need a different crystal to answer questions from each area. It is OK you if need to switch crystals as you read about each aspect of your life.

It is also OK if you hold the same crystal throughout the whole process. It will be a good reminder that you can remain the same person in all areas of your life and thus become closer to your integrated self.

This idea of integration is better than seeing life as fragmented in these areas. In reality, these areas are facets of the same crystal, which is your life. They are all one. What we want to do in life is to feel the energy of joy, love, and truth integrating and permeating all these areas or facets and creating a flow of well-being that runs through and connects them all.

Observing these areas of life from a perspective of integration is always better than living each of these aspects as separate from the other, and separate from you.

As you observe these areas of your life as facets of the same crystal, and after you've finished the whole process of answering the questions in all areas of your life, you may want to do it again with another crystal, and it will be a totally different experience.

The crystal you choose to hold can sit anywhere whenever you are not reading the questions and answering them. No need to do anything special with it.

So once you have chosen your crystal, you are ready to start answering the questions about the first area, which is your physical body.

After you have answered the questions about your physical body, I suggest you wait a day or at least a couple of hours before you move on to the next area (your financial life).

You do not have to ask yourself these questions all at once. Take your time. They are deep. My suggestion is that as you hold your crystal, you read all of the questions and observe how you feel before your start answering.

Then, waiting a little before you answer the next round of questions allows the unconscious mind—which has been gently stirred—to be ready for the next layer for accurate observation. And you can move on to the second area, and then to the third, and so forth, waiting a little before you start each new round of questions.

Just remember the best awareness results will come if you allow yourself to rest and digest these questions before moving on to the next set. This is advice I give you from previous experience and my research.

The only areas that seem to be OK to be done sequentially and digested together are financial life and professional life, but sometimes they can be a big deal for some people, so you will know what makes sense for you.

If you spend a day with each area, after you have answered the questions, try to let them sink in without judgment. Be kind to yourself. Your current situation and the present moment are not fixed, unchangeable structures. If you are not living the best of lives, there is always a possibility for change.

Now you are ready to start. You will observe your body, your finances, your home, your professional life, your emotional life, your unique self, and your spiritual self, in this order.

Let's begin.

Your Body
Remember to hold your crystal as you read these lines and answer these questions.

There are two important things to observe in your physical body: health and image.

Believe it or not, your body is an accurate image of what goes on in your emotional life and in your soul. If you are happy with your body and you are a healthy person, that gives you a good idea of how your emotions are and in what state your soul is.

If you feel there is something you do not like about your body, it is important to be aware of which emotions are causing you to feel that way. If you struggle with health issues, find a health care practitioner and do not postpone going to a medical doctor.

If you are interested, you can also find a holistic health care practitioner to try to observe with you what kind of emotional and soul imbalances may be contributing to the fragility of your health. But do not substitute holistic health care for traditional medical doctors if you have serious health issues.

When we observe image, in our Western, industrial, mass culture societies, the appearance of the physical body has become a huge source of identity and a reference of self, according to external, subjective beauty standards. Of course the body is important for many reasons—it gives us a sense of self and experience of an individual life. But nowadays it has become a huge source of anxiety, and the image of the physical body has been exaggerated as a crucial source of identity.

If our physical bodies do not match specific standards of weight, height, body shape, eyebrow size, etc., and if it is not dressed in specific types of outfits, many people have low self-esteem and feel as if they do not belong. This can really mess up their sense of self-worth.

The physical body could be a fun source of expressing yourself and feeling the pleasure of being alive, but in many people's lives, it has become a stress factor. People start living from the expectations of the outside world instead of living from the heart. Instead of enjoying the journey in the physical self in joy and self-care, a lot people worry too much about living up to external standards of beauty and image.

In many cases the health of the physical body has become a second priority compared to aesthetics. When the body becomes a vehicle to certain standards of beauty and image instead of an end in itself as a source of life, health, and well-being, something is wrong. We can almost guarantee there is something unhappy about that person, and it affects quality of life too.

With this in mind, it is time to observe how you feel about your body. In order to understand where you are right now, ask yourself these questions:

1. Is my physical body *healthy* and happy? Or do I have symptoms, diseases, and discomforts?
   a. If so, in which areas of my body do I have symptoms, diseases, or discomforts?
   b. Do I seek professional help to take care of my physical body (medical doctors, dentists, complementary healing modalities), or do I ignore the pain and the symptoms?
2. Am I happy with the *appearance* and *image* of my physical body? Do I think it is beautiful? If not, why not?

    a. What could be better in the appearance of my physical body?

    b. Do I seek professional help to deal with the subjective discomforts caused by the image of my physical body (psychological therapy, energy healing modalities, life coaches)?

Let your answers sink in and digest them. Observing these areas of your physical body can be emotional for some people. Take your time and observe how you feel.

Rest a little if you need to (remember to hold you crystal). Allow your awareness to expand and deepen itself.

If you decide to wait a day or just a couple of hours, when you feel you have digested the answers to these questions, you are ready to look at another dense level of your life, which is your home.

Your Home

Where you live is a major area of your life, and how you feel about your home plays a great role in your well-being. Our immediate environment must ideally be clean, beautiful, bright, and as natural as possible. Being close to nature is very important, not only for our physical health but also for the happiness of our souls and spirits.

Take your time to observe your home and how you feel about it. Observe how you felt in the months or years you have lived there and what you like most about it.

With that in mind, hold your crystal and ask yourself the following questions:

1. Am I happy with my home? Do I love it? Is it nice? Is it clean? Is it pretty? Is it close to nature? Is it close to the places I need to go on a daily or weekly basis? Is it close to work and friends?

2. Am I happy with the situation of my current living? Are the financial arrangements of my home something I have deliberately chosen to best fit my needs? Could things be better in terms of rent, mortgages, and owning my own home?

Ask yourself these questions as you connect to the reality of your home, taking your time to digest the answers. Hold your crystal in the process. Follow your intuition and don't rush yourself. Let the answers sink in.

How you relate to your home is a very important and profound dimension of your life, so respect this process fully. Pay attention to your feelings about your answers.

After a day or a few hours or minutes, you can step into the next area of your life, which relates to your finances.

Your Financial Life

Remember to hold your crystal as you read these lines and answer these questions.

As an adult human being, it is important that your financial situation is comfortable according to your standards. This is a subjective issue, and no one but yourself is able to understand exactly what kind of budget and financial life you want to have.

Since people have very different ideas about what they need, there is no right or wrong in this matter. Each one of us hopefully knows what we want and what we desire.

It is also very important to observe where your income, money, and financial streams come from. Do you provide for yourself, or does someone else provide for you? If you rely on someone else to provide for you, or for part of your everyday living, is this provider a husband, wife, or life partner? Is this person a brother or sister? Or is this person someone older like a mother, father, grandparent, or uncle?

If someone else provides for you, there is balance if that someone is a husband, wife, or life partner. Marriage always means you have moved forward in life, and couples balance themselves in different ways, financially or otherwise. However, if a sibling or someone older than you, like a mother, father, aunt, uncle, or grandparent, provides for you in adult life, part of you in your unconscious mind still behaves like a child.

If your inner child is secretly in charge of your life, and as an adult you are still financially dependent on parents, siblings, or older family members, your inner child is winning the game. The inner child still has more power over your life than your adult self.

It does not matter if you are 18, 24, 34, or 64 years old. Inner child ruling can go on forever in an adult person's life if there is no awareness and no will to change. This can shift with awareness and positive focus with inspired action, if that is what you are truly willing to do.

Observe if there is peace of mind in your current situation in regard to money and your finances. For some people (not everyone), being provided for as an adult is uncomfortable. For others, it is great. It depends on the person.

If you have a nice, comfortable financial life, do not work, and have a life partner to provide for you, it really has everything to do with what your needs and desires are when it comes to money and professional success and ambition. As I said earlier, there is a difference if the provider is a parent or some other family member, or if it is a life partner.

Couples have different ways of balancing themselves. In general, if your material life is provided by marriage, it means you are less dependent and less in child mode than someone who is an adult and still provided for by parents or other family members. This is not a judgment; it is just a way to seek clarity about who runs the show and who you want to have your life conducted by—your inner child or your adult self.

After you have observed your current situation about money, hold your crystal and ask yourself the following questions:

1. As an adult, am I financially independent? Do I have more than one stream of income? Do I rely on someone else to fully or partly provide for me (parents, grandparents, aunts, uncles, husbands, wives, or someone else)?
2. Is my financial life OK?
   a. Do I have debt?
   b. Am I happy with the amount of money I make, or could I be doing better?
   c. Do I desire a more prosperous, financially abundant life?

After you have finished answering these questions about your finances, see if you need some time to digest the process or if you are ready to observe your professional life.

These two areas can be intrinsically knit together, but in Your Cardinal Connections, they are seen separately. A person may have a good, stable financial life, but it does not mean it is provided by a job or by that person. This person might not even have a professional life or be married, and another adult of the family might support this person. Other times, the person has a great financial life and provides for himself or herself, but makes money in an occupation he or she hates, so professionally the person is not happy.

Let's understand the basic principles of a professional life.

Your Professional Life

Remember to hold your crystal as you read these lines and answer the questions.

The most important thing to observe about the financial and professional areas of life is the guilt factor. Guilt ruins your happiness and frequently permeates financial and professional lives.

A lot of people feel guilty about making money because many members of their family struggle financially, and they feel bad about being successful. Others feel guilty about pursuing unorthodox careers, so they settle for traditional jobs and end up feeling miserable and guilty about not allowing themselves to be professionally happy. And others feel guilty about not working because they have wealthy life partners, husbands, or wives, who provide for them enough so they do not need to work.

If you are happy being provided for by your husband or wife and do not feel like your inner child is running your life, that is great. Do not let external standards rule and dictate your well-being and how you should feel. As part of a couple in an adult relationship, you may behave in ways and provide other types of energies that make your partner happy with many of his or her needs, so you are in balance.

The biggest frustrations related to money and professional life usually are:

1. *Feeling guilty* about being supported by a life partner
2. Providing for yourself by leading a professional life you hate
3. Not being able to provide for yourself and being supported by parents, other family members, or governmental unemployment policies

With that in mind, you can answer the following questions:

1. Do I need a professional life to be happy? If so, do I have one?
2. Am I happy in my professional life? Does it provide me with enough financial support to satisfy my basic needs and desires?

Hold your crystal and take a deep breath as you answer these questions about your professional life. After you have finished answering them, observe if you need to digest this new awareness or if you are ready to move into another crucial aspect of your life, which is your family, your relationships, and your emotions.

Your Emotional Life
Remember to hold your crystal as you read these lines and answer these questions.

Your emotional life is greatly determined by your childhood and what you have experienced as an individual. However—and here's the catch in the perspective of Your Cardinal Connections and The Cardinal Method of Life Connection—our unconscious minds are also greatly ruled, usually much more than by our individual experiences, the emotions of our parents, and the emotions of our ancestors.

When it comes to understanding Your Cardinal Connections, it's vital that you assimilate this principle—a lot of your emotional life is ruled not by your individual emotions, but also by the emotions of your mom, your dad, your grandparents, sometimes aunts and uncles, and sometimes even older siblings.

This is a fairly new concept to our Western culture and has been revealed and explored in the field of family constellations, a therapeutic modality designed by Bert Hellinger. If you want to know more about family constellations, The Cardinal Method of Life Connection is very inspired in this modality, and there is a video I recorded on my YouTube channel that explains the basic principles:

https://www.youtube.com/watch?v=283A0cmznek

We will also discuss this topic further in this book, and there are other in-depth references to search for if that is something you are interested in. We have some references in the last pages of this book too.

The fact that the emotions of your parents and ancestors matter a lot to your emotional life is very important to understanding your own feelings. They are combined with your own feelings and affect the quality of your friendships and of your romantic life.

Being aware that your parents' and ancestors' emotions affect your life may encourage you to be more mindful of the delicate, intricate web of feelings that create your emotional life. As you let this information sink in, hold your crystal and think about your mother, your father, and at least your grandparents before you begin to answer these questions:

1. How is your relationship with your mother? Is/was she a happy person?
2. How is your relationship with your father? Is/was he a happy person?
3. How do you feel about your grandparents, aunts, and uncles?
4. Do you have deep, nurturing friendships? Do you have many friends and acquaintances, or few friends?
5. What is the quality of your romantic life? Did you ever have painful breakups?
6. Are you frustrated in any way for not having lived a romantic story with someone?

7. Are you in a stable relationship right now? If so, are you at peace, or is your heart still broken from past relationships and unfinished love business?

After you answer the questions about your emotional life, digest your answers for a while. Be mindful that you are getting in touch with not only your individual emotions but also with how you feel about your parents, grandparents, aunts, and uncles.

Let the answers be observed by your higher self. Take your time, as long as you need.

After you have processed your emotional life (we will come back to that later in this book), you can look at a very objective and powerful aspect of your life that determines a lot of your experiences—your thoughts, beliefs, and brain power.

Your Brain Power
Remember to hold your crystal as you read these lines and answer these questions.

Our thoughts and core beliefs determine our emotional states. We basically have two types of contents in our brains: beliefs about others and ourselves, and objective information and knowledge about the world that allows us to be fulfilled and independent professionals and citizens. Both types of content are extremely important for Your Cardinal Connections.

To understand more about your brain power, you will keep reading this book, and it will start to open your mind in areas that were once blocked or resistant to a more fulfilled life. The reason I say this is because a lot of people do not even realize that their self-worth is deeply compromised and limited by strong depreciation of self in thoughts and subconscious beliefs that undermine their happiness.

There is also a lot of room in the brain that could be used to accumulate useful and objective knowledge to help not only ourselves but also humanity to live better lives. However, we either waste this potential with limiting beliefs or we do not have the urge to seek self-improvement or personal growth.

Ideally we should be using our brain power to discern limiting and toxic thoughts from objective, positive thinking. When we can do that we are already way ahead in the game. Another very important step is accumulating useful knowledge with clarity so we can create wonderful things in the world with our hearts. This is not always the case in many people's lives, and understanding Your Cardinal Connections may help with that.

The intention here is to start to bring awareness to the areas of your brain that are clogged with limiting belief systems, so that your mind can literally breathe. In order to start doing that, you can answer the following questions:

1. What are your thoughts about yourself? Do you depreciate yourself in any area of your life, such as your body, your finances, your job, or your relationships?
2. What are your thoughts about the world, and what area interests you professionally? How do you think applying your useful knowledge can create good results in the world and make you, your community, and humanity happier?

Observe how you feel about your brain power. Maybe you started to break away from limiting beliefs and self depreciation. Maybe you have obtained more clarity just by answering these questions. Take your time to digest what came up in your answers.

After you have answered and digested the questions about your brain power, you are ready to move on to the deeper and higher levels of your self and your spirituality.

Your Unique Self and Your Spiritual Life

Remember to hold your crystal as you read these lines and answer these questions.

Your unique self is Your Cardinal Connection that makes you an unrepeatable individual in humanity. It is where your inner child and your ego reside. It also involves your life purpose, your personality, your dreams and desires, and what you create in the world.

Your inner child and your ego are not good or bad, as many people may think nowadays. These two aspects of our psyche have been misunderstood in a lot of ways. The inner child and the ego have a dual nature, and they may manifest their healthy side or their wounded, distorted side.

When the inner child is hurt, we tend to be either submissive or rebellious, and sometimes selfish, resentful, dependent, and superstitious. When the inner child is happy, we tend to be spontaneous, loving, and allowing and open to life. We take ourselves lightly—and we especially know how to have fun.

When the ego, which is the rational, independent, adult aspect of the psyche, is hurt, we tend to be perfectionist, intolerant, and omnipotent, and we have a very amplified image of ourselves as powerful. Some people may have a God complex to save the world or think they are very important, often surrounding themselves with people who operate in victim mode so they can feel powerful.

When the ego is healthy, we have a positive focus in life and create good results for the self and for those around us. We become good observers of ourselves and the world, and we develop a disciplined way of living that brings feelings of peace and freedom. The healthy ego knows exactly when love is flowing from a healthy source and when distorted feelings are disguising themselves as love and admiration. The healthy ego, most of all, tends to remain neutral in silent observation.

With the aspects of your unique self in mind, it is important to understand two things. The first is that you need to have a clear picture of who you are as an individual. The second is that, from that clear picture, no matter what has happened, you focus on the beautiful aspects and potentials of your being so that you always love and respect yourself as an individual.

When you have a clear picture of your unique self, it is time to understand the highest and most evolved part of who you are—your spiritual self. Your spiritual self has always remained pure and untouched by distortions.

The spiritual self is different from the unique self because it is pure Love, pure Truth, pure grace, and pure freedom. These energies can be called essences of life, which are not unique to specific individuals—they are present in each and every living being, in all human beings as beautiful potentials.

We are all coming from a natural state of being when we express Love, grace, Truth, and freedom. It is a state of bliss that some people connect to and others do not. Different people connect to these essences of life on different levels.

This is a part of ourselves that is very similar to crystal energy, because crystals are very pure. They also have the power to activate the higher self or spiritual self, and they can encourage you to not only manifest your best aspects, but also energize all of your other cardinal connections.

Think of your higher self, your spiritual self, as pure love and grace, joy and freedom. Hold your crystal and feel the energy of who you truly are.

With this in your mind and in your heart, ask yourself:

1. How would you describe your personality, your dreams, and your aspirations? Do you have a clear picture of what they are?
2. Do you respect yourself and pursue your dreams and aspirations? How much does your life clearly mirror who you really are and what you really want?
3. Do you consider yourself an introvert or an extrovert? Are you an introvert but were forced by family, school, life, and circumstances to become an extrovert? Is the opposite true (you were naturally an extrovert and were forced to become an introvert)?
4. Do you respect your personality and your nature?
5. Do you meditate? Do you pray? Do you connect to a spiritual higher self?
6. Do you have a spiritual practice you are consistent with every day or every week?
7. Are you living a life according to Love, grace, Truth, and freedom? Do you come from a place of purity when you connect with other people? Have you ever connected to the life essences of Love, grace, Truth, kindness, and freedom and manifested them in your life?
8. Which one of these life essences seems hardest? Which one seems easiest?

Answering these questions gives you a clear picture of your personality, and you can start developing respect for your unique self and who you really are. This clears the path for you to get in touch with your spiritual self. The spiritual self is deeper than your personality, and it also gives you a broader perspective of who you really are.

Take deep breaths and hold your crystal as you allow the answers to sink in. Try to stay silent for a while after you have answered these questions. Closing your eyes and lying down a little bit can be very good after this process.

Congratulations on finishing this part of the process and for your trust in the shifts that this awareness will bring. You're just beginning, and this is already a huge step.

Since you have answered all the questions about Your Cardinal Connections as you held your crystal, you now have a better picture and a more panoramic view of your life. Your awareness is growing, your mind is expanding, and you will begin to get flashes of consciousness in how to tune into simple, practical solutions to your problems. The presence of crystals inspires these energies in our lives.

Slowly and permanently, as you strengthen Your Cardinal Connections, you will see your life become a river of flowing, abundant energy.

And as you slowly get rid of blockages, entanglements, confusions, doubt, fear, stagnant energy, anger, and frustration, your paths will open to new worlds of wonderful possibilities. Life will begin to move forward with more ease and a lot more joy—and these are, precisely, the typical energies that Your Cardinal Connections and crystals bring to you.

3

YOUR SOUL

To strengthen Your Cardinal Connections, it is very important to understand what the soul is. Hold your crystal and pay attention to some of the things we are about to address together in this chapter.

Understanding the soul is important so you can heal it. There are several different ways to describe the soul, but in essence, it is an aspect of yourself that seeks wisdom, connection with a higher purpose, and evolution.

It is not uncommon to see the soul's purpose being unclear to many people or clashing with distortions of the inner child or the ego. When that happens, we get frustrated and thrown out of balance because there are blockages to fulfillment and joy in the inner child, the ego, or the soul, or in two or even all three of them together. It can get confusing.

The soul is very sensitive and gets hurt very easily. When the soul gets hurt, it needs to be healed and repaired. If the soul tries to heal on its own, it will usually try to do that by unconsciously attracting and repeating situations of emotional pain so that it can either compensate injury or overcome it. Neither strategy (compensation or repetition) is efficient because they both lead to more pain and never bring a satisfying solution.

The soul is different from the spirit or higher self because the soul has a story, a history really. Like the spirit or higher self, the soul is a nonmaterial and a very real aspect of your self. However, while the spirit is and always has been an aspect of God within each human being, the soul has an evolutionary process and began with humanity, evolved with humanity, and is part of our human experience.

In a big-picture perspective, the soul is a mass of energy, experiences, and emotions with a past, present, and future, and it evolves with generations.

There is an individual soul within each person, and there are collective souls as well. A collective soul is not something we have but something we belong to, like embroidery on tapestry or icebergs in an ocean. In these examples, each person is a part of an embroidery in a majestic tapestry, and the collective soul is the fabric. Whatever happens to the fabric affects all embroidery in the tapestry and vice versa. The same goes for the iceberg image. The collective soul is the ocean, and the people are icebergs floating around, made of the same water, belonging to the same ocean, but in a solid state of ice instead of water.

The most powerful collective soul we belong to as human beings is our family soul. We also belong to other collective souls, such as all the groups of people we are part of. Every group of people that is ever formed creates a collective soul. The largest souls we belong to are our cultural souls and the soul of humanity, which are very strong too.

When we try to understand the logic of collective soul, the most important idea to have clarity about is the feeling of belonging. We belong to our families, to our cultures, to our cities and countries, and to humanity.

The most powerful collective soul we belong to in a state of unawareness is our immediate family—mother, father, and siblings. The family soul is defined by sharing the same blood, the same history, and the same present moment.

With this in mind, it is important to understand that the soul is:

1. Both individual and collective, being our family soul the strongest of all collective souls we belong to
2. Very sensitive and easily impacted, because the soul is *emotional*, while the spirit is joyful
3. Open to healing, if we take charge of our own self connection and awareness processes. We can help purify the many collective souls we belong to with individual inspired actions

What happens in our contemporary Western cultures is that we do not know these perspectives and we do not have this information. Bert Hellinger, the creator of Family Constellations, brought this knowledge to the Western culture from what he learned from the Zulus in South Africa.

In our Western culture, our rational conscious minds are so controlling and encouraged to take over life and explain everything with rational concepts, that most of us are disconnected from the deeper emotional aspects of life and from the soul. And since emotions and the soul cannot be rationalized, they are shoved away to the realms of the unconscious areas of our minds and rule our lives from the subconscious without our conscious awareness.

To understand more about the soul and how it is present in our lives, remember to hold your crystal as you read the next pages.

Your Individual Self
If the soul is collective, how can it also be individual? How do we know the difference between our individual soul and the collective souls we belong to?

Our individual self is a multifaceted being. The individual soul is one of these facets or aspects. The collective souls we belong to (such as our nuclear family, our ancestral family, our community, our culture, and our humanity) are other facets or aspects of our being. They are different layers of our psyche, different aspects of us, that together add up and create our unique individual selves.

An individuation or integration process happens when these different aspects merge into one with conscious awareness and connection to the heart. We then become more integrated and fulfilled individuals—which is what happens when someone like you starts to expand your consciousness and are interested to learn about Your Cardinal Connections.

You will live in the present moment and flow at ease with life much more frequently if you commit to the process of self-connection and expansion of awareness, and allow the integration of the different aspects of your self to happen in their own timing.

Many books and many experts will give different names to these layers of your psyche or aspects of your self. To strengthen Your Cardinal Connections, you will connect yourself with the main aspects of your being, which are your inner child, your ego, your individual soul, your spirit or higher self, your conscious mind, your heart wisdom, your free will, your collective soul, and your immediate family.

Let's understand what each of these aspects of your being is.

Your Inner Child

The inner child and the soul are very emotional and sensitive. When they are imbalanced, they tend to be fragile, addicted to drama, and overwhelmed with trauma or painful experiences.

The focus of the inner child and of the soul (both individual and collective), if left to their own devices, tends to be in painful experiences from the past and in trying to heal those past wounds. The inner child is stubborn, and the soul seeks wisdom and evolution by attracting and overcoming painful experiences.

Both the inner child and the soul tend to react from a place of emotional pain and not from creativity when they are hurt. They need the help of our conscious awareness and higher self to overcome these tendencies and merge into a more integrated version of who we really are.

Your Ego

The ego has a different nature when compared to the soul and the inner child. It is rational and objective, and when imbalanced, it is usually the rigid and controlling aspect of us that tends to shut off emotions and make life as functional as possible.

The ego can shut down our emotional lives and close our hearts so we can perform well in adult life, but that leads to unhappiness and a sense that life has no meaning.

The ego has a sense of responsibility, and if it serves the higher purpose of the spirit, it fulfills its mission. When the ego wants to control everything, it not only becomes frustrated with time, but it also tends to make our lives miserable.

Your Individual Soul
As explained before, your individual soul has a history, a past, and a future, and is very sensitive. Since it gets hurt easily, you can heal it with spiritual practices and emotional connection with the help of therapists and with a mind-set that frees you from victim mode.

Ideally, the individual soul realizes itself when it becomes pure like your spirit, and this is another reason why crystals can help you in this journey. They bring their purity to your individual soul and help it clear itself from distortions and painful memories.

Your Spirit or Higher Self
The spirit or higher self is a spark of infinite joy that is ever-present inside your heart. It is a life source within your self.

The spirit makes life meaningful and full of purpose. It does not know anger, sadness, depression, fear, worry, anxiety, or attachments. It is immune to any kind of emotional poison, and it can literally be described as the presence of God within you.

Your Conscious Mind
Our conscious minds are important parts of who we are. Without them we would never be able to think logically or understand the world.

The conscious mind and the ego should not be seen as the same thing, even if they have similarities. The conscious mind is a functional aspect of our lives, and the ego is an existential aspect.

The conscious mind is a functional aspect of the mind, and unlike the ego, it is not aware of any existential issues.

The nature of the conscious mind is to compartmentalize and discriminate everything so it can understand life in its smallest particles.

It needs very specific concepts to understand the world, and it does not have a very expansive or integrative nature.

It wants to discern good and bad, right and wrong, and many other dualistic aspects of life for a better understanding of the world. If the conscious mind is the predominant aspect of who we are, we get stuck in compartmentalized, rigid, dualistic mind-sets, and we see the world from that limited perspective of separation.

When someone has a predominant conscious mind that does not accept a spiritual life, does not care about the physical body as a source of well-being, and dismisses emotions as unimportant, this person is likely to be unhappy. Unfortunately, we see many people in our culture with that way of thinking, who live in a general sense of frustration with a limited life.

This is why it is important for us to develop a strong, healthy conscious mind along with other aspects of our being, such as caring for our physical body, our emotions, and our spirituality. When the conscious mind is able to share space and connect to our other human dimensions, our quality of life is much better.

Your Heart Wisdom
Unlike the conscious mind, the heart has a harmonious, integrative nature that connects us to all there is. We need both the conscious mind and the heart to become whole and to integrate ourselves with our bodies and our spirits.

The wisdom of the heart brings kindness, compassion, and generosity to our lives, starting with ourselves and expanding toward others. Love of self allows us to genuinely love others without attachments, neediness, or emotional compensation agendas.

All human beings are capable of feeling this loving kindness and connection. Ultimately, all life connections begin and end within your heart. It is the home of *Your Cardinal Connections.*

Your Free Will
With your free will you make choices in your life, but they may be motivated by unconscious distortions or connected integration.

Your free will manifests at its best when you feel integrated and in peace.

It manifests at its best when you are happy in your body. It manifests your best efforts when your conscious mind is active and intelligently expanding toward higher and more qualified knowledge, and you find yourself searching constantly for good education and creative processes.

It also manifests your virtues when your heart is connected to your true needs and desires and you feel harmonized with other people's truths as well. This can mean you are aware of potential conflict with whatever is not aligned with your truth, and you can make a choice to discern what serves you and what does not.

From this perspective you know you have the freedom to connect your life with specific people and not with others, which is fine if it expresses the Truth of who you are.

Your free also manifests its best potentials when you understand that a spiritual life is important and gives meaning to life, and that spirituality can manifest in many ways and not just in obvious ones. You do not have to be religious to be spiritual, as Oprah Winfrey once said. Being spiritual means you are connected to the truth and to human virtues. The idea is not to force an obvious idea of spirituality, but to understand and feel what is true to you and respect the subjective truths of other people.

Your Collective Soul: Understanding the Groups You Belong To
Aside from having an individual self, which was described above in many of its aspects, we also belong to groups that build up our sense of collective soul.

Your collective soul is made of the groups you belong to, especially your immediate family—parents and siblings, grandparents, your extended family of aunts and uncles and cousins, your neighborhood, your city, your culture, your country of origin, and the countries where you have lived.

We are very influenced by the lives, emotions, and experiences of our ancestors, and they are part of our collective soul too.

I will now describe some of the ways our sense of collective soul can be imbalanced by the history of our ancestors and parents and by our sense of belonging to groups in general. Collective belonging affects our individual psyches and emotions and sometimes determines a lot of our life experiences.

Your Immediate Family
Obstacles to the flow of life can happen when, as children, we sense there is something not so pleasant or distorted going on with our parents. The tendency we have as children to deal with this emotional perception is to develop unconscious fantasies that we can somehow solve our parents' problems or save our parents from emotional pain.

This is a childish fantasy of omnipotence, and children make unconscious promises to fix whatever is emotionally wrong in the parents' lives and later live their adult lives according to this unconscious promise.

Regarding the collective family soul, it is important to understand that wherever there is lack of love, that is exactly where the loving, blind love of the child will develop a fantasy of omnipotence and try to save the day. The inner child of many people may still be ruling their lives from that fantasy. This means that when a child reaches a certain age, as a teenager or as an adult, that child will live similar painful experiences as part of the fantasy and unconscious childhood promise that was made to save the parents.

For example, one of these fantasies is to emotionally console an unstable, needy, or hurt mother or father. This will lead this child to search for love partners that have the same emotional pain as the parents when this child becomes an adult. If the father was an alcoholic, the child will attract an alcoholic husband, for instance. This person may attract complicated relationships because in the mind, this person is saving the parent as the childhood experience of sensing the parent's emotional pain is projected on the partner.

According to Jakob Schneider, the most common ways to observe this kind of unconscious behavior is when adult individuals live their lives in one or more of the unconscious programs he describes as compensation for painful experiences in the collective soul. These compensation strategies can exist on their own or combined with each other. Schneider describes some of them as consoling emotionally needy parents, developing emotional partnerships with one or both parents, interruptions in the flow of affection, judgment and recrimination, depression, and spiritual escapism.

I will explain what each of these situations involves, but keep in mind that these issues are generalizations from experience and years of collecting data in family constellation practice and literature. They are not intended to explain the path of your life or make your personal experience fit into generalizations, but these may be powerful guidelines for you to observe your psyche and your emotional life.

Hold your crystal as you read each of these situations and observe if they make sense to you and if they remind you of people around you.

If you see other people in these situations, hold your crystal tighter and make a commitment not to judge them or impose information on them. At the most, kindly suggest that they read this book, but do not be pushy.

Your focus should be on your own life. If you find yourself observing someone else's behavior instead of observing yourself, you may be engaging in avoidance and sabotaging *Your Cardinal Connections*.

Consoling Emotionally Needy Parents

If your mother's childhood was sad, she may not have received enough love, care, and attention from her parents (your grandparents) or from one of the parents.

Since children are full of love and feel a need to create loving atmospheres wherever they are, when they sense there is lack of love in the family, the inner child may unconsciously try to fill that space, or void, with his or her own love. But if the void is created by the sadness of your mother as a child, filling the void with love was your grandmother's job and not yours. Your mother's inner child needs the love of her own mother, and you as the daughter or son cannot ever make up for the lack of motherly love, simply because *you are not your mother's mother.*

Children have no idea of hierarchy when it comes to the family soul. They have a blind kind of love that goes wherever there is lack of love, and they do not care that the love parents and ancestors' need is specific and that they cannot fill in the voids created by older family members.

Since for the soul there is no time and no space, your mother may not be a child anymore, but emotionally there is still a wound or void of that active emotion, that feeling of lack of love. As her child, you energetically sense that wound in the soul and try to fill it with your own love, creating confusion.

In practical terms, when your inner child is trying to take care of emotionally wounded parents, as an adult you may be taking energy away from a crucial area of your life. This may bring difficulty to that area of your life. If you are unconsciously doing that, your focus is not in the present moment, in your job, or in creating and prioritizing your own family. You may be emotionally taking care of your mother, trying to compensate for the absence of love created by your grand-mother. And that never works and does not solve anything.

If this is your case, the big leap in your life will happen when the inner child within you realizes that giving your mother the love that she needed as a child *is not your responsibility.*

The emotional state of the person who takes emotional care of a mother or father is called *inversion of the flow of life energy.* Your moth-er's emotional job is to give you love, and your emotional job is to receive love from her, and not try to give it back as if you were the mother and she were the child.

You can, of course, love your mother *as a daughter or son.* The problem is when a child's psyche is disorganized by the blind love and tries to take emotional care of the mother, making efforts to be present for her as her own mother should have.

An example of this situation is when a woman spends a lot of her time being very present with her mother and keeping her company, in an unconscious effort to make up for the lack of love in her mom's childhood. Some daughters never get married or leave home because they're caught in this emotional entanglement. When this type of situation is seen in a Cardinal Method of Life Connection family constellation process, a lot of release may happen and major life shifts will follow.

With this in mind, hold your crystal and ask yourself if any of these hypothetical situations describe your life in some way. Sit for a moment with these thoughts and let them sink in before you move on to the next description.

Developing Emotional Partnerships with One or Both Parents
Another type of distortion in the flow of life energy within families is *partnerships in different generations.*

If, for example, a child realizes that her parents are unhappy in their marriage, out of blind love and the omnipotence complex, that child may try to make up for the lack of love felt by one or both parents in the marriage. Children are *very* sensitive to the Truth, no matter how well adults try to hide it.

This means that in fantasies, the child may unconsciously try to become the ideal partner for the mother or father (or both) in an effort to keep the parents' marriage stable. The child becomes a shock absorber and juggles around to keep the parents happy, forgetting about the child's own life and happiness and directing all emotional energy into the parents' marriage.

If, for example, the father feels his wife is emotionally distant or does not have enough in common with him, and wishes his wife were different, the daughter may mold herself to become exactly the ideal wife for the father, even if that creation is far from the truth of who she really is.

The father may wish his wife were an artist and she is not. The daughter is intrinsically an intellectual, but she senses her father would love an artistic wife, so she does not develop her intellectual talents and becomes an artist instead to please her father. In an attempt to hold everybody together as one happy family, her childhood fantasy of omnipotence may speak louder than her own truth and her own happiness.

With this in mind, hold your crystal, think of your mother, and ask yourself if you do things to please her that contradict something that would please yourself instead. Does your mother appreciate certain ways of acting and being that are not expressions of your true self, and not really part of you, but you unconsciously become that person anyway to make her happy? Do you prioritize what your mother likes instead of what you like?

Do the same exercise with your father. Hold your crystal and ask yourself if you would rather please your father than please yourself in some or many areas of your life.

If the answer is yes to any of these questions, regarding both parents, there is some sort of family loyalty in you that is not allowing life to flow as abundantly as it could.

The problem with this dynamic is that this child, and later this adult, may live life trapped in the entanglement of the parents' relationship—and be unaware of it. Instead of making the child's life and wishes and desires a priority, that child is making the mother's or father's preferences a priority and possibly living an unhappy or unfulfilled life.

Interruptions in the Flow of Affection
According to Jakob Schneider, interruptions in the flow of affection happen when a young child is physically separated from the mother or father at an early age. In my experience I have seen that this can happen because the parents got divorced when the child was very young, or one of them died or left home, or the child was given up for adoption. Interruptions in the flow of affection and abandonment can cause a lot of damage to a person's unconscious mind and encourage emotional fantasies of compensation.

This physical separation creates emotional distance. Some people feel like part of them is missing because this physical connection between parent and child has been interrupted at an early age.

Not all people who go through separation from one of the parents at an early age develop this issue of interruption in the flow of affection. However, if some area of your life is deeply imbalanced and you have gone through separation from your mother or father at a very early age, this might be one of the unconscious root causes of your present life's problems.

An area of your life may be blocked from consciousness, and your drive to manifest good things in the world may be weak. You may have difficulty in relationships or in creating a family, pursuing a happy professional life and career, having financial abundance, or coping with chronic health or chronic pain problems. There is no rule.

Hold your crystal and observe if an area of your life seems like it could be charged with more energy and fulfillment if you gain awareness about separation and dissolve this blockage by under-standing your inner child's pain.

Also observe how you feel about abandonment and interruption situations. Sometimes one of the parents traveled a lot or worked long hours and you rarely saw him or her. Usually separation refers to very real physical absences like divorce or death, but sometimes people develop the interruption in the flow of affection unconscious block-age because they did not get enough physical presence from one or both parents, or because the parents were physically present but emo-tionally distant.

Judgment and Recrimination of Parents
When we focus on our parents' personalities and their lack of pres-ence or love, instead of focusing on the fact that they gave us life, we engage in judgment. This causes major damage to our soul because it is an arrogant state of consciousness that does not acknowledge life and gives energy to our parents' flaws instead.

Arrogance toward our parents diminishes the grandiosity of life that has been given to us through them. When we judge, criticize, or recriminate one or both of our parents, consciously or unconscious-ly, we almost automatically take the second step and develop uncon-scious guilt. When judgment and guilt coexist in our psyches, they often feed each other, and our hearts short-circuit because there is no flow of life energy in this vicious cycle.

It is important to make it very clear that guilt will always, 100 per-cent of the time, make you attract self-sabotaging experiences in your life. With this in mind, hold your crystal and understand that if you judge your parents, you will be engaging in an unconscious dynamic in which your soul knows you're being arrogant and ungrateful, and that will trigger conscious or unconscious guilt, which will in turn attract self-sabotaging experiences into your life and create a very uncomfortable vicious cycle, whether or not you are aware of this.

In a more visible way, not accepting your mother's and your father's flaws and personality problems may also interrupt the flow of love and affection in your life in general. Sometimes this happens when we receive so much from our parents that we lose the point of reference where it all began—they gave us life, which cannot be compared to anything else.

Also, judgment may come when we receive too much from our parents. We become spoiled and unclear of core life essences, and we tend to turn our focus to superficial things and find a reason to criticize our parents instead of being grateful for the life that has been given to us.

The best way to deal with judgment is to focus on the essence of life, which is life itself. Life is the best gift we can receive, and anything we get beyond that is more than a blessing. So when you hold your crystal and internally thank your parents for the life they have given you, instead of looking at their personality flaws and judging them, you will become whole.

Depression

According to Jakob Schneider, this happens when the child feels that one or both parents have so little energy and so little to give that they do not take any emotional energy and support from them. This type of child will have difficulty receiving good things from the world because she did not receive and did not dare take anything from the mother or father, for fear of depleting them from the little energy that they already had.

Depression may come because this person, as an adult does not know how to receive the good life. This leads to emotional exhaustion and depression.

If you feel this may be your case, hold your crystal and observe in which generation the strength of life may have been interrupted in your family. If one of your parents did not receive enough and you felt that if you took any energy from them they would be depleted, take deep breaths and bring this possibility to your awareness as you hold your crystal.

You may feel you need to seek a good therapist to talk about this issue.

Spiritual Escapism

According to Jakob Schneider, there may be certain spiritual or religious practices, groups, and meditations that spiritually separate children from their parents and that disrupt the flow of life energy. They are sophisticated ways of not accepting the parents as they are.

This perspective affirms that life is too grand for our parents to create it, and that it comes from higher sources. This is true on some level, but our biological parents are a crucial part of this process and coauthors in the life that has been given to us. To deny this is to interrupt the gratitude flow and to focus on the limitations instead of focusing on gratitude, regardless of our parents' flaws and personalities.

When we proclaim spirituality as life on its own and do not honor our parents and ancestors, we lack strength and tend to have a confusing and unfulfilled life, often engaging in denial mode.

Hold your crystal and observe if you on some level relate to spiritual escapism and deny your family roots. Observe how you feel about this information as you take deep breaths and allow your awareness to expand.

Your Siblings

According to Family Constellations literature and empirical observations in family constellation fields, the bonds between siblings are very strong—possibly the strongest bonds in the unconscious mind. We feel very connected with siblings because we have the same physical origins as they do—our mother and/or father.

This loyalty can be very explicit and obvious or highly unconscious. There is a lot of unconscious loyalty among brothers and sisters, even if they fight and do not speak to each other for years. In these cases, loyalty seems unlikely, but deep down it is there. If brothers and sisters are fighting and not speaking to each other, the loyalty is there because they are together in the same pain, and there's no escape from this type of bond in the perspective of Your Cardinal Connections.

The fact is that siblings naturally love each other and feel very connected. If, however, they have personality conflicts and are fighting or not getting along, the flow of life and love is interrupted, and their quality of life decreases immensely. It is very painful to the soul when siblings do not speak, and this is because it is natural for brothers and sisters to love each other. When that does not happen, suffering is inevitable.

For your awareness, hold your crystal and observe how you feel. If you have siblings, think about your feelings toward them and their feelings toward you. Observe how you act with them. Observe if there is harmony, neutrality, or no feelings at all. If you feel nothing, there is probably blockage.

Observe if there is a feeling of conflict or discomfort. Just being aware of how you feel about your siblings will already start shifting your life. Hold your crystal and send love to your siblings. Even if it does not seem true to you, do it anyway.

By sending love to your brothers and sisters, wherever they are, alive or deceased, your life will start to flow into better directions, and you will find the emotional quality of your days increase in peace and well-being.

Your Ancestral Family

Your relationship with your mother and father are key factors for the quality of your emotional life. The same goes for your siblings. However, in our culture we do not seem to realize how much the life experiences of our grandparents and great-grandparents, and also of aunts and uncles of their generations, are transmitted to us through our parents and also influence our lives at deep levels.

More frequently than not in my professional experience, I see highly sensitive people with an omnipotent inner child who is tuning in to the generation of the grandparents or aunts and uncles in their emotional pain. This is what Jakob Schneider calls *skipping the parents*, and the latter is what I call *diagonal identification,* meaning people connect in a diagonal line with aunts and uncles instead of connecting in vertical lines with parents and grandparents.

Since the abundance of life flows in stronger currents through vertical lines, when you are too identified with the life experiences of aunts and uncles, your life may not be as great as it could be. Also, sometimes (less frequently, but also significantly) I see people tuning in to problematic experiences of great-great-aunts and great-great-uncles too.

To expand your awareness, if you can investigate the lives and experiences of not only your parents and grandparents but also of your aunts and uncles from past generations, you may find out that some of them had hard lives. Some of them may have gone through traumatic events or painful experiences, such as loneliness, untimely deaths, complicated diseases, tragedies, bankruptcy, abandonment, and many others.

Your unconscious mind is already born with all that information, which may or may not be charging your life with your relatives' traumatic experiences without your awareness. If your life needs improvement in many areas, and you find out those aunts and uncles of past generations had painful lives, you may develop unconscious identification in a diagonal line of family loyalty.

If that is a possibility, hold your crystal and think about it. Think about the information you know about ancestors in general, including aunts and uncles. See if you can ask older people in your family about their life stories and the stories of your ancestors. See if you can find pictures of ancestors who had painful life experiences. If you find them, place a crystal on their picture for one day and then clean your crystal under a water faucet or on dry sea salt. This will help you with your peace of mind.

Your Cultural Soul and Group Belonging

Now that you have a better understanding of your immediate and ancestral family, you can hold your crystal to understand more about your cultural soul and group belonging.

Aside from belonging to your immediate family, which consists of your parents, your siblings, your aunts and uncles, and your grandparents and great-grandparents, you also belong to a cultural soul.

The cultural soul includes religious belonging and national belonging. Your culture, religion, and nationality determine part of your emotions and guide your unconscious mind much more than you realize.

The city you were born in is also very important. We are emotionally impacted by the environments that surround us and also by the environments that surrounded our ancestors. Our connection to the city we were born in gives us strength because it is part of our roots.

For example, I was born in Brasilia, Brazil. My father's family is from the states of Amazonas and Rio de Janeiro in Brazil, and his great-grandparents were from Brazil, Portugal, Italy, and Switzerland. So my ancestral paternal family had a strong connection with Native American cultures of Amazonas and also different cultures in Europe. Consequently, unconsciously and emotionally, I belong to all those places and cultures too. Even if they seem far from me, in a distant past, they are actually very present and very real in my psyche.

I have less information about my mom's family, but I know they are from the states of Bahia and Minas Gerais in Brazil, and in a more remote past, from Portugal and Italy—and those Italian ancestral family members left Italy for Portugal as far as we know. So I belong to all those countries and states too.

Since for the soul time and space do not exist, the reality of our unconscious mind is that different time frames and different geographical locations overlap and exist in parallel within our psyches. They are all very real in the present moment and have not vanished with the passing of time. They are here, in every cell of our being. Portugal, Italy, Bahia, and Amazonas were the reality of my ancestors, as they are my reality too, because in my family lineage, that's where I come from and that is part of who I am.

So you can see how broad our cultural and geographical connections are and how we belong to so many different places when we think of our ancestral families combined.

Hold your crystal and think about your ancestral cultural lineages. Take deep breaths and close your eyes. Realize you belong to a much broader spectrum of realities than you ever imagined, and silently, if you feel an open heart, thank your ancestors and your parents for your life.

4

FRIENDSHIPS AND LOVE RELATIONSHIPS

*T*he *Pathwork of Self Transformation* says that "above all else, life is relationships." In the perspective of Your Cardinal Connections, friendships and love relationships are very important because they create new life and new happiness in the world.

Unfortunately, a lot of people feel vulnerable in friendships and love relationships, and a lot of confusion, misunderstanding, and painful experiences are present in this area of our lives. This is because we have unconscious emotional charges that trigger fear, anxiety, and anger from time to time, and those who are closer to us may suddenly feel like threats.

To learn more about how and why these emotional charges trigger our psyches in destructive ways, I suggest you read Eckhart Tolle's book, *A New Earth: Awakening to Your Life Purpose*—specifically chapter five, titled "The Pain Body."

Our emotional wounds in friendships and love relationships can be healed. Hold your crystal as you take deep breaths and observe the following explanations.

With mindfulness and an open heart, the ability to observe the truth with the help of crystals can help you harmonize your relationships. For broken friendships and painful love relationships, it is very efficient to practice the Hawaiian Ho'oponopono prayer, which can be used for any problematic area of your life.

Considering Your Cardinal Connections, your love life and your friendships play a huge role in your emotional health and in your soul, both individual and collective.

Before you observe the next aspects of love and relationships, hold your crystal and connect yourself to your heart and to the inner truth of whom you love and whom you have loved in the past. Observe how you feel when you think about these people.

Then you can tune in to important friendships that still exist in your life and those that ended. Think about everyone who is important to you right now and how everyone you love or have once loved has a place in your heart.

Do this in your own rhythm. As you hold your crystal, observe the friendships and love relationships in chronological order so that you engage both your feelings and your rational mind in the process.

Start with dear childhood friends. When you are ready, move forward in time and think of teenage friends and your boyfriends or girlfriends. Think of all your friendships and love relationships in your twenties and the years that followed.

Take a deep breath as you hold your crystal. You are now ready to observe each person with the understanding of Your Cardinal Connections. As you hold your crystal, read on and observe how you feel.

Friends
Our friends are very important to us and are a great part of Your Cardinal Connections. Healthy friendships play a big role in life and emotional well-being.

Think about your friendships in childhood. Did you have good friends? Was there trauma with friendships? We you bullied, or were you a bully yourself?

Take deep breaths as you access those memories. Observe how you feel as you hold your crystal.

When you are ready, think about your teenage days. Are you still in touch with your teenage friends? Do you feel you have a lot of friends or very few?

The number or friends and acquaintances does not mean there is a right or wrong way of living your friendships. It simply shows your nature, so you may be an introvert who has fewer friends on deeper levels, or an extrovert who has a lot of friends and needs a bigger variety and intensity of social contact.

Extrovert people need an active social life and nurture themselves by social contact and by constantly being with other people. To extroverts, being alone is usually not very fun, and it can be painful and even energy depleting.

Introverts, on the other hand, nurture themselves by spending time on their own in silence, near nature or in a cozy environment. This is very soothing and replenishing to them. Social contact is nice but in small doses and usually with a small number of people. Too much social contact can be draining to introverts. They feel as if they are giving their energy away and nurturing others with prolonged social contact.

Hold your crystal and observe if your friendships are nurturing and fulfilling or if they are draining. Also observe if you feel yourself as more of an introvert or an extrovert.

Observe if there are friends you no longer see and that you wish you had more contact with. How do you feel when you think of them?

Hold your crystal and observe if there are broken friendships that you feel you may never be able to restore again. You may or may not want to restore this friendship. Take a deep breath and allow the truth to come clearly to your heart.

If you feel you may want to reconnect with the person, visualize the friend you once had and send love from your heart without expectations. If reconnections should happen, they will come naturally.

Hold your crystal and do the same with an old friend you clearly feel you may not want to reconnect with again. Be mindful of your boundaries and do not feel guilty if you decide not to reconnect with that person. Visualize the friend you once had and send love from your heart, allowing the friend to go.

After you have done that, touch your heart with your hands and acknowledge the friendship. Let your feelings be expressed without judgment. Observe if you can feel grateful for the good times you shared with friends you wish to bring back to your life and friends who you do not wish to reconnect with.

If you cannot feel grateful for the good times, repeat this exercise as many times as you feel is necessary in your own timing. It does not have to be right away. Respect your emotions and keep reading.

Example #1: How Maria and Samantha Drifted Apart

Maria and Samantha had been very close friends since high school and in college. They both enjoyed poetry, literature, music, art, and ancient history. As young adults, they decided to go to the same college and were still very close.

However, Maria's boyfriend at the time met Samantha and did not like her very much. He thought she was too clingy and eccentric and too much of an introvert. It is true that Samantha felt Maria was her best friend, and she did not need many more friends to feel fulfilled. Samantha also had complicated relationships with her boyfriends and her family, and she was especially harsh with her mother.

Maria's boyfriend thought Samantha was not a good influence, and after they had been dating for a year, he told Maria he thought she would be better off with more "normal" friends and should start hanging with his friends' girlfriends more frequently. He also told her she should not be so available for Samantha; otherwise, she would never really grow up.

Maria had her own emotional issues and was so afraid of losing her boyfriend that she did not oppose him. She slowly grew apart from Samantha. Even though their friendship fulfilled her soul in many ways, the thought of conflicts between her boyfriend and her friend led her to pick sides. Maria eventually followed her boyfriend's will instead of taking time to observe how *she* felt about her friend and the alleged limitations her boyfriend thought she had.

Samantha was devastated with the friendship slowly dissolving. Maria was never clear and upfront with her because she didn't have the nerve to tell Samantha the truth. Maria was sad, but at the time she did not have the strength to really connect to her emotions and blocked her heart from feeling all the pain she needed to feel. She dismissed her sadness as unimportant and focused on maintaining a good relationship with her boyfriend.

Samantha thought that if Maria did not have enough discernment on her own to figure out how manipulative and emotionally abusive her boyfriend was being, it was not up to her to warn her friend.

She did not want to be accused of ruining the relationship with her judgment and did not want to be accused of jealousy. She kept to herself, and the two friends grew apart, never speaking to each other again.

In this example, Maria prioritized her boyfriend's feelings instead of her own, and Samantha decided that if Maria revealed herself as a weak person, the friendship was not worth risking her image in coming forth and warning her friend about her emotionally abusive boyfriend.

Maria pushed her sadness aside, and it was shut off in her unconscious mind. Samantha was hurt, angry, and judgmental. She was very aware of her anger and kept feeding it resentment as time went by.

Five years later, Maria and Samantha are still not speaking.

Maria ended her relationship with that boyfriend two years after she grew apart from Samantha, but she never reconnected with Samantha again. Aside from being ashamed, she thought making an effort to reconnect with Samantha would be too much of an emotional effort, and she was too focused on other problems to make that happen. Samantha was still angry and did not want to reconnect with Maria anyway.

The two former friends have emotional wounds in their souls. If one of them decided to heal those wounds, both would benefit because the energetic connections between their hearts still exists. If one or both of them decided to heal, they would not have to become friends again but would reconnect with the truth of their emotions, release the emotional pain, and experience a great sensation of relief.

Exercise A: Healing Friendships
In friendship situations, true healing does not necessarily come from physically reconnecting and reestablishing a new friendship with the same person. This can happen, but it does not have to. Healing can occur regardless of reestablishing a friendship.

What you can do to heal the friendship individually in a Your Cardinal Connections perspective is, first, hold a crystal as you take deep breaths. Second, acknowledge the truth of what happened in your heart and take responsibility for your actions, feelings, interpretations, judgments, thoughts, and decisions.

As you do this, observe how you feel about the other person in the present moment, and decide to do what your gut and your heart tell you to do, whether it is trying to reconnect with the person or letting go. Whichever path you chose, remember to make your decision with loving compassion for yourself and for your friend.

This last step—the decision of what to do about it: reconnecting or letting go in peace—may take a while. Meditating on the situation and especially holding a crystal in the process of decision can do wonders for the emotional healing of your friendship on the soul level.

If you have unfinished business or a painful situation with a friend, try this exercise. You will see how peaceful and healed you will feel afterward.

Platonic Love

Platonic love means you have once loved or liked someone, but you have never touched or had a love relationship with that person.

This can be more serious that we think. Unfulfilled love is an unsettling energy that instigates our curiosity and consumes a lot of energy, especially if it happened when you were young. It takes you away from the present moment because it fuels the inner child's tendencies to escape into fantasies of the past. It can also disturb committed relationships in the present and disturb your peace of mind.

Platonic love and unfulfilled fantasies hurt the soul and block emotional growth. When these feelings linger into adult life, you may feel a constant mild frustration in the undercurrents of your mind. Life in general may seem tedious. Since we do not associate this feeling with the nurturing of fantasies and platonic love, we do not really understand our lack of energy.

It is a very subtle mechanism that seriously takes away energy from the present, from your projects, and from your life. Little by little, it may also undermine your self-esteem in the long run.

To better understand how destructive platonic love can be, hold your crystal and read the following story.

Example #2: Juliet and José

When Juliet first saw José in her first year of college, she liked him right away. She liked his overall energy, and as she got to know him, she liked him more and more. He was kind, good looking, honest, committed to his work, smart, disciplined, charismatic, and a little shy, which she thought was adorable.

Juliet wanted to get to know him better and go out with him. The more she observed and interacted with José, the more she liked him.

The kinder José was, the more Juliet nurtured feelings for him. She began to think José was a perfect match.

But after a few weeks Juliet found out José had a girlfriend back home, and she was very disappointed.

Juliet began to withdraw. Instead of interacting with José naturally, she began to distance herself. José was a little puzzled with her change of behavior, but he did not bother to ask if anything was wrong. He did not know her that well, and he had other priorities in his life.

Juliet never told any of her friends she had feelings for José. Aside from being shy, Juliet did not want anyone to judge her. In her mind she imagined people would think she was unethical for liking a committed guy.

But her feelings for José remained. She cultivated them in her heart and began to convince herself she loved him, even if nothing had ever happened between them.

Throughout the years, Juliet kept that idealized image of José in her mind like a treasure. She did not have a chance to get to know him enough to even know if he was all she imagined him to be. She never had a relationship with him, so she never got to see his flaws and imperfections. She just convinced herself that he was perfect.

Because Juliet kept nurturing feelings and an idealized image of José, she had boyfriends that always had a resemblance to him—either in their looks or in personality traits.

Juliet and José went their separate ways, and each got married and had children with other people. However, Juliet's heart still beats faster whenever she hears anything about him from mutual friends or sees something about him on the Internet.

Though she got married to a very nice man and had children with him, she never got over her fantasies about José, her college acquaintance, and her quality of life was never very fulfilling because she was not emotionally present in her own reality.

Exercise B: Releasing Platonic Love
Platonic love is an unresolved emotional issue. Unless we bring an objective perspective to the picture, we will never allow ourselves to let go and be fully present in this very moment.

The problem with not fulfilling or not even trying to fulfill emotional desires is that they grow inside of us and tend to be exaggerated by our imagination. Platonic love then becomes stagnant energy in the soul.

If you feel this resonates with you on any level, hold your crystal and make a list of all platonic loves you once had. Think about each special person you remember, picture that person in your mind, and if there is more than one, think of each separately, one at a time. Observe if you still nurture fantasies about that person.

Then, as you hold your crystal, say out loud: "(Person's name), I love you. I acknowledge the love I once had for you, and I acknowledge it was never fulfilled. You will always have a place in my heart. I now let you go because my own life and my peace of mind are my priority."

Take a deep breath and wait as long as you need. Keep breathing slowly, in and out. Think of your breath as a process of letting go.

You may feel shifts and releases in specific areas of your body as you do this, especially the heart and lungs. Then say, "(Person's name), I let you go."

Do this exercise as many times as you feel are necessary, with as many platonic loves you feel were important in your life, until you feel your heart is lighter and your breath is flowing in peace and well-being.

Remember to always hold your crystal as you do this exercise. This is very powerful and effective for soul healing.

Unfinished Love Relationships, Breakups, and Divorces

Our emotions are wounded and our souls are torn apart when we have painful breakups, divorces, or unfinished love relationships (when one of the partners breaks off communication and disappears).

When one of the partners takes off without communicating to the other partner that he or she is leaving, and this interrupts communication, there is a huge wound in the soul. This is also true in friendships. When a person simply abandons the relationship and never communicates again, the abandoned partner suffers great emotional pain.

Abandonment is one of the most painful experiences anyone can go through. The pain of being abandoned by a love partner can be compared to the pain of being abandoned by one or both parents. It creates trauma in the heart and in the soul.

When, for example, your boyfriend or girlfriend disappears, or shuts down, or interrupts communication, and you still had some issues to resolve and needed a longer closure process, that experience is also felt as abandonment.

When communication is interrupted, the heart begins to close itself. This happens with the person who has abandoned and also with the person who has been abandoned.

Observe if this is happening between you and a former significant other, even if the relationship ended years ago. Unfinished emotional business may still be active. Some things may still need to be said on your side, and they have not been said because the other person has made himself or herself unavailable.

This could also be your case—maybe you have abandoned someone or made yourself unavailable to communication.

Either way, it is painful for both of you, and both hearts are wounded in the process of abandonment or being abandoned.

Abandonment is worse than rejection, because rejection has more clarity and is more connected to the truth of the heart. Abandonment is an expression of a confused mind and a confused heart and expresses no clarity of what the Truth is.

Abandonment in love relationships is different from interruptions in communication with family members. People who deliberately stop talking to their parents and/or siblings also create emotional pain, but it is a different kind of pain.

In families, your individual freedom to make choices in this life is not as consciously involved as it is in love relationships. We are bound to family members by blood, and we choose our love relationships with our hearts. Interruption in the flow of affection with family members is a blood and soul issue. Abandonment in love relationships is a heart and soul issue.

Love relationships are expressions of freedom. The relationship existed because of personal choice and not immediate blood ties. It feels different, and that kind of pain of abandonment in love relationships tends to create self-hate if we are not careful and aware of our emotions.

Self-hate, in this case, has to do with a tendency to blame ourselves for not choosing wisely. We blame ourselves for giving our hearts to the wrong, undeserving person—someone who did not honor the relationship, who did not honor our love, and who has decided to shut down communication and run off as if we were worth nothing.

Aside from abandonment, breakups and divorces are extremely painful too, especially if one of the two did not want the relationship to end. Even if you wanted the separation or divorce to happen and felt relieved with the breakup, if the other person is still in pain, your heart will feel that pain too because the connection is very strong and the relationship belongs to both of you.

If the other person is still suffering and you are not considerate of that situation, your life flow will be slower than it could be, even if you do not connect the dots. Your life may even be a little blocked because if the other person is still in pain, it resonates in your heart. This creates unconscious guilt in the heart, and you will not feel completely liberated. It is not easy for either person in the relationship if one of the two is still in pain.

To understand how this works, hold your crystal and read the following story.

Example #3: Clarissa and William
Clarissa and William fell in love in adult life after both had established their careers and were independent financially and professionally.

They both had good educations, good jobs, good financial lives, and their own homes.

They decided to get married, and Clarissa found a place for them to live. It was a beautiful house near the woods with enough room for guests and children. They had been dating for four years, and it was the perfect place to start a family. William helped her pick some items for the house. and things seemed to be on a roll for a great start.

However, a few months before their wedding, William began to distance himself and his behavior changed. Clarissa felt her heartbeat accelerate more than usual, and in her gut she felt something was wrong. Her friends kept telling her marriage is a big shift and it was normal for him to act weird, and that it would pass once they tied the knot.

William was acting more distant as days and weeks went by. Clarissa's heart was telling her something was very wrong. She decided to talk to him about it, and William admitted he was not ready for marriage.

Clarissa's heart sank. She could not believe William was backing off after all the emotional and financial investments they had made together. All the plans and promises. All the investments. Not to mention how much she wanted to have children; her biological clock was ticking and he knew it. Now the whole world seemed to be collapsing under her feet.

She felt horrible and undervalued. She hated herself for choosing the wrong person—a man who did not want to marry her, who did not value her, and who did not care about her worth. In her mind, she could not have made a worse choice in her life.

She screamed and cursed and shouted and called William horrible names. She wanted to destroy his self-esteem and ruin his life because he had just destroyed *her* life and torn it into pieces. He apologized in the beginning and said he was very sorry, but Clarissa's verbal aggressiveness grew worse, and he got so mad he withdrew even more, disappeared from her life, and never spoke to her again.

Clarissa and William went their separate ways and never heard from each other again. After ten years they are still not speaking, and when one thinks about the other, there is still bitterness, anger, resentment, and a feeling of unfinished business in their hearts.

Exercise C: Healing Painful Separations
Breakups like this can be as painful as divorce for the heart and soul. If there is still active negative emotion in the hearts of the two people involved, it is very toxic to their hearts, to their souls, and to life in general.

Not all breakups or divorces end with bitterness. Sometimes they can bring huge relief, and the ex-partners remain friends. However, if you have experienced abandonment, painful breakups, or divorces, emotional pain is still in your heart, or in your ex-partner's heart, or both. If this is the case, this exercise will be good for you.

Hold your crystal and think about your ex-partner.

Feel what is going on in your heart. Allow all energies, pleasant or unpleasant, to surface.

Take deep breaths. Maybe you will have insights and new awareness. Maybe what needs to be understood will be clearer just by sitting down, holding your crystal, and breathing while you think about your ex (or exes) with whom you had painful breakups. If there is more than one, think of them one at a time, and do this exercise for each one separately.

Get a piece of paper and write a letter to this person. Keep your crystal close to you.

When you finish writing, burn the letter outdoors and observe how you feel.

If there is more than one unfinished love business, you may even use a different crystal for each person, maybe even with different colors and shapes. From my observation of clients and friends with this practice, holding different crystals with different colors and shapes is usually a good idea, especially if the ex-partners were very different people.

Interestingly, a lot of unfinished love business seems to have a pattern, and we often observe similarities in behavior or traits between ex-partners of the same person. It is almost as if they are different songs playing on the same radio station. If you feel there is a pattern and that you need to hold similar crystals, follow your intuition and do it.

Think of one specific ex-partner. As you hold the crystal, breathe for a few minutes. Take deep breaths and take your time. These steps need to be taken slowly. Do not try to rush through the process to get it over with because it is painful. Feel the emotional pain as you hold your crystal. You can handle it.

Keep thinking about your ex-partner. After breathing in and out as you hold your crystal, you will probably have an intuition about what happened on a deeper level. If the relationship ended, what are the hidden benefits that your anger and hurt do not allow you to see? How can you be relieved about the breakup? Remember that life is wise and that if you had gotten married or remained together, it might have been worse.

Keep taking deep breaths. Be mindful of your body and how you feel physically. As you breathe and hold your crystal, you will get more insight about what you should do about the nasty breakup or divorce right now, in the present moment.

You may feel you need to write another long letter and then burn it to let all the emotional pain go. Maybe you do not need to do anything—you can just let go in peace. Maybe you will need to try to make contact with the person in a kind, civilized way, if your heart feels relief when you think about this course of action.

As you breathe and hold your crystal, be mindful of the difference between impulsive action and inspired action. This is why you need to sit with each breakup story separately and take your time.

If you feel you need to contact the person, sit with this idea for three days before you make that contact. Try not to be attached to it. Try not to resist it either. Breathing and holding the crystal will help you get clarity. As Dr. Ihaleakala Hew Len says, if the idea persists for three days after being mindful, act on it and see what happens.

Understand that the results are not important. The process of action to release and let go is what really matters. Do not worry if the person does not answer. Keep breathing and focusing on your intention to let go of the emotional pain.

Focusing on whatever seems to be unfinished emotional business with your heart will bring you relief and clarity about why the relationship ended. It will bring you more acceptance about why things happened the way they happened and why they are the way they are today.

You will especially have more clarity about which steps to take next. If it is letting go, let go. If it is a communication attempt, as long as it is an *inspired action focused on letting go*, do it. And always remember that breakups, painful as they may have been, more often than not are blessings in disguise.

When we are clear enough from the emotional pain of your past, we are able to engage in mature, fulfilling, healthy new relationships that bring love, joy, and personal growth to your life. I know this exercise works, and I truly hope it is as effective for you as it has been for me and many of my friends and clients.

The Magic of Committed Relationships in Healthy, Happy Marriages

If you are in a committed relationship, hopefully it is a healthy one.

A good way to check if you are in a healthy committed relationship is if you feel free and at ease with yourself, if you feel spontaneous and you do what you like, and especially if your breath is deep and strong as you inhale all the way in and exhale all the way out.

If you are too attached to your life partner or feel insecure in the relationship, there is a problem. Also, if you feel bored in your relationship or marriage, it is also a problem. A healthy committed relationship or marriage does not share space with attachment or boredom.

If attachment or boredom is in your life with your partner, honestly observe how you feel. It does not necessarily mean you are with the wrong person. It just means you may need to look deeper within yourself to gain more awareness. Starting with *Your Cardinal Connections* is a good way to do it. Observe what needs to surface to your awareness about the relationship and which honest adjustments need to be made in your heart and soul.

When you are in a relationship, *always* connect to your feelings and observe yourself constantly. The whole purpose of commitment is to feel joy and fulfillment as you and your partner grow and expand together in love and freedom as independent adults.

Healthy, happy marriages are possibly the most fulfilling spiritual experience a person can have, but if you feel like marriage is not for you, it is OK. Most human beings find their emotional and spiritual fulfillment in a long-lasting, happy committed relationship though, and if this resonates with you, keep reading this part of the book and do the exercise.

The first thing about a fulfilling, strong relationship is *balance*. In order for your relationship to be fulfilling and happy, one partner cannot behave like a parent or a child of the other partner. Independent, healthy adults treat each other with love and respect in a horizontal perspective. If you feel your partner behaves like a child and you like a parent or vice versa, that may be comfort zone for you, but the underlying currents of your emotional life are probably far from ideal. You may be secretly dissatisfied, bored, or exhausted.

If you behave like a child with your partner on one or many level, try to observe this and see how you feel. This is another comfort zone temptation that does not allow you to live life to its fullest potential.

A happy, healthy adult marriage is a symmetric, fulfilling relationship—a constant, mutual expansion of joy and personal growth. Ideally, both partners are financially stable, professionally realized, and emotionally supported by friends and family, and have developed self-worth and self-esteem.

In the book *Alchemy of Love Relationships*, by Joseph Michael Levry (Gurunam) says that when a couple is truly united in love and freedom, their relationship is not a third party in their lives anymore. Instead, picture two droplets of water merging together and becoming a bigger, single drop of water. You feel complete and whole with the other person. A happy, healthy relationship feels like home.

Before you check the story of a successful, committed relationship, do the next exercise and observe how you feel. You will understand, on a deeper level, how Your Cardinal Connections can work in the full potential as they are naturally manifest themselves in your life.

Take a deep breath, hold a pink crystal (it can be any pink crystal, such as rose quartz, pink mangano calcite, danburite, morganite, rhodochrosite, or any other pink crystal, as long as it is pink), and start.

Exercise D: Connecting to the Magic of a Happy Committed Relationship
Lie down and close your eyes. Hold the pink crystal in either hand and take deep breaths.

Imagine your heart as a heart of pink crystal. Picture a glowing pink light surrounding it. Hold your pink crystal and allow this image to become very vivid.

Keep breathing deeply while holding your pink crystal. Imagine your partner's heart made of a pure pink crystal and visualize a glowing pink light around it too.

If you do not have a partner, imagine a strong, pleasant person with a heart of pink crystal and a pink light surrounding it.

Keep breathing as you hold your crystal and imagine both pink crystal hearts merging into one. Imagine a pink light expanding and surrounding your body and your partner's body.

Take deep breaths and allow the image of this big pink crystal heart to become very vivid.

Keep breathing and say, "I love you." Imagine your partner responding, "I love you."

Now visualize this pink crystal heart pulsating. Take deep breaths and smile.

Hold your crystal and imagine your whole body surrounded by pink light.

Open your eyes, place your crystal on your heart, and continue breathing until you feel you can open your eyes in gratitude and positivity.

Example #4: Your Story
Instead of reading about the examples I can give you of happy, healthy marriages, you will now write your own story. This is a story you will tell in this book.

You can make it up or write your own experience. If you've never been in a healthy committed relationship and would like to be in one, make up your story with an open heart and allow all the best energies in you to surface—happiness, joy, love, peace, and fulfillment. As you write, you will start to create your life as a happy one.

If you are in a committed relationship and it is not so great, write down what you do not like about it and how that could improve. Here is the most important part of this exercise—each flaw you see in your partner needs to be written down next to a flaw you see in yourself, and next to the description of the flaws, you will write down what can improve these issues.

When you write about your partner's flaws and your own flaws, they do not have to be the same, but they may somehow match in resonance. For example, I hear a lot of women complaining their husbands are aggressive, but they on their turn are not assertive when the husband is aggressive; they are passive instead.

This creates a distorted balance in the marriage. If the passive wife were more assertive in creating her own healthy boundaries, there would be no space for the husband to be aggressive.

I also see a lot of women complaining that their partners are too quiet, and not surprisingly, the partner will complain that the wife in turn is too loud. Another common situation I see frequently is that one partner is lazy, but the other is hyperactive.

These are not symmetric relationships, and the couple stays together in the distorted balance or in compensation of flaws. This does not mean things cannot improve, but it takes awareness, love, and commitment for that to happen.

Since this is a book about Your Cardinal Connections, and it starts with awareness of self, when you complain about your partner, it is an indication that you do not see something within you that triggers that unpleasant behavior in the other person.

Observe how you process this and do not beat yourself up for it. Judging and being unkind to yourself will interrupt the flow of healing. Hold your crystal and just be mindful of your self-observation as you write your story.

As you hold your crystal, look back at the descriptions of Your Cardinal Connections. Create two characters that are in a loving, happy, healthy committed relationship, preferably you and your partner. If you do not have a husband or wife or serious relationship, imagine yourself and an imaginary partner that would be great for you.

If your partner is imaginary, be very careful about not choosing someone you know or a movie star because you do not want to interfere in someone else's energy free will. Imagine someone you have never seen before, and if Your Cardinal Connections are in a good state and improving, life will bring a good person to your experience.

Do not try to control who that person will be or look like. If we commit to healing with integrity, life will always provide someone better than we could have ever imagined with our limited minds.

The reason I am encouraging you to write your story as an example is to give you confidence in creating your own life and so you start getting used to this idea. In the perspective of Your Cardinal Connections, *you are the creator of your own life.*

Hold your crystal, start imagining your story, and write it down.

Forget about perfection and just do it. Write down whatever comes to your mind spontaneously after you have done the previous exercise.

Hold your crystal, get a pen or pencil, and start creating:

_____

_____

_____

5

YOUR LIFE'S PURPOSE AND THE IDEA OF GROUNDING SPIRITUALITY

When you feel happy and at peace with yourself and the world, you are on the right track to fulfilling your life purpose.

That feeling and that path bring joy, inner peace, a sense of self-connection, and a positive focus in life. When performing the right activities for yourself and sharing your life experience with people you love, you develop a mind-set that life is great. You feel wonderful and sober because you have a pure, positive mind-set, and you also feel grounded and responsible for all areas of your life to function properly.

This feeling does not have to be very enthusiastic all the time. It is not euphoric. It is vibrant and peaceful at the same time. Though it is full of energy, it is far from being intense or delirious. It brings you peaceful optimism and the desire to expand your knowledge; connect to other people in loving, productive ways; develop nurturing, reciprocal relationships; and enjoy life's endless possibilities and opportunities for personal growth.

When we feel vibrant and full of life, we manifest good things in the world and contribute to humanity in joy and well-being. We live in a state of *grounding spirituality*, which is a result of your alignment with Your Cardinal Connections.

Grounding spirituality means you manifest good things in the world with sober awareness and responsibility. You are not just lying around reading theory and preaching love and peace, talking but not acting, or simply reading books. You are actually living from inspired action and manifesting the beautiful potentials of life in the world.

You are also going one step further than just knowing the theory. You are practicing principles of integrity and manifesting your creativity as life's endless possibilities for growth and expansion.

You may or may not be a spiritual or religious person, but that does not matter in the perspective of Your Cardinal Connections and grounding spirituality. People who are happy and bring good things to the world and humanity are already living in grounding spirituality.

Sometimes these people are religious, and sometimes they are not. People with a closed heart may call themselves spiritual just because they believe in God, but they may treat others badly or live in denial and avoidance of emotional pain. When the heart is closed to other human beings, connection with higher realms simply does not happen.

People can sometimes be bitter, cruel, and unproductive. If someone you know is like that, it is likely that they have closed their hearts to one or more of their cardinal connections. This type of person can drain other people's energies. This does not mean they are bad people—it just means they are in emotional pain and are not doing much or anything about it. Sometimes they are not even aware that their hearts are closed.

One of the ways to avoid being awake, aware, and connected to life is by engaging in spiritual escapism. If you know someone like this, do not judge this person. Try to look at this person with compassion because that lack of awareness may someday change.

Do not preach about self-connection or Your Cardinal Connections or try to change that person's life. There is nothing more annoying than imposed help. We should only give help, even in advice, if someone explicitly asks for it.

Imposing your help on others can have the opposite effect of what you intend. It may create resistance. When people's emotions and souls are ready, trust the flow of life and know that their paths will shift. They, too, have free will and their own timing.

If someone deliberately comes to you for advice or help, be there for them. Be mindful of your own boundaries and never deplete their energy with excessive advice. True nurturing of self and others comes when there is a reciprocal flow of energy and both parties feel at ease.

If you want to understand the idea of *grounding spirituality* in the perspective of Your Cardinal Connections, observe yourself and see if you are already practicing it.

Grounding spirituality is a path or way of living that integrates honoring the memories of the past and letting them go, focusing on the present moment and consciously engaging in productive activities and in your personal spiritual growth.

It also has a sobriety to it in which you do not compare yourself to other people, and you do not engage in judgment of self and others.

Grounding spirituality is a result of committing to Your Cardinal Connections, and it is a process that evolves into an upward spiral of expansion. You will lead a spiritual life that integrates all aspects of your life.

Start by taking consistent baby steps. They will evolve into an expanded spiral with your commitment to create a routine of mindful breathing, constantly holding a crystal to remind yourself of Your Cardinal Connections and feeling peaceful and confident as you explore new modalities for personal growth, create authentic relationships, and develop your talents.

Honoring the Past and Letting It Go
Honoring the past means you have consciously decided that regardless of what happened in your family history and in your own individual experience, you have chosen to live in the present moment and to move forward into a good, happy, healthy future.

For that to happen, you need to let go of all emotional debris. There is no such thing as moving forward without letting go.

Some of your emotional debris may be shoved away in the darkest places of your unconscious mind. To clear it out, do the exercises described in this book.

This does not mean you need to be an enlightened human being without any emotional charge from the past. It just means that if you commit to observe yourself constantly and have the discipline to keep a positive focus in life, you will create a good life with your heart's positive energies.

When you shed light and love on the wounds of your emotional history, you acknowledge them, make peace with them, and take the strength from your history instead of carrying the weight of past pains.

Focusing on the Present

Focusing on the present moment is the key to a good life. When you focus on the present moment, you realize that the family past does not belong to you. You also realize that your own memories are not that important anymore.

You take care of your own life and create it in happiness and joy, doing your best to live in a way that makes you happy. You fulfill your dreams, wishes, and desires, and they manifest without much effort when you are in the positive flow of life.

Using Your Free Will to Engage in Personal and Spiritual Growth

One of the best ways to engage in personal and spiritual growth is through mindful breathing, silence, and creativity. Being aware of yourself and of your heart's wisdom in conscious silence is a very effective path to personal growth and to developing grounding spirituality.

Try to practice being silent for a few minutes every day as you breathe deeply. Practice being mindful of who you are and of the environment around you.

As you practice silence and breathing, you also practice your creativity. Allow it to flow into the world in its happiest manifestations. When you are creative, life flows and the whole world benefits. Your light shines within, and your spirit or higher self will finally run the show.

Letting Go and Moving Forward

I hope understanding Your Cardinal Connections has been a good journey for you, as it has been for me.

As I observed each one of my Cardinal Connections in my inner world throughout the past fifteen years, I have made movements that strengthened these connections and made me more aware of my life. I made steady progress any many areas and my path has become brighter, more meaningful and more beautiful over the years.

This has been my experience, and sharing it in a book is an honor, a pleasure, and a joy.

Since the best way to manifest good intentions and creativity is through practice, in the next two chapters I will show you the practical steps you can take to live Your Cardinal Connections in their fullest potential. Now that you know the theory, enjoy the ride of the practice. Let's flow!

6

HEALING YOUR INNER CHILD

I f you remember from Chapter 3, most of the problems we have in life involve two aspects of ourselves: our wounded, reactive inner child and our controlling ego.

The emotionally wounded inner child we all carry within is, most of the time, active in our unconscious minds and may be ruling our lives without being noticed.

The wounded inner child causes problems such as self-sabotage. It makes you want to be taken care of instead of being independent. It has a need for instant gratification at the expense of health and peace (such as overeating, not exercising, overspending, being irresponsible about money and bills, not cleaning the house, and missing and being late for appointments, among other behaviors). The wounded inner child does that so you and other people will pay attention to its endless, unfulfilled needs.

To understand how your inner child is affecting your life with unconscious emotional demands, observe if you are attracting unpleasant events to your life. I recommend you read *The Pathwork of Self Transformation* by Eva Pierrakos to get more familiar with this subject.

I also recommend you do this practice in order to observe your inner child. Understanding the mechanisms of your wounded inner child brings awareness to your life, and you will not be trapped in its strategies to remain in control of your life anymore.

The practice I have developed for Your Cardinal Connections is an exercise with a stone bracelet and a crystal. It is very simple and fun because it brings awareness, relief, and well-being to your life while including your inner child and setting healthy boundaries instead of punishing it. You can do it by yourself, and it only takes ten minutes.

This practice can be done every day. Let's flow with it.

Inner Child Self-Healing Practice
Create a healthy space for your inner child in your life by connecting to the joy of living. The joy of life is all any child in the world wants anyway.

A healthy inner child radiates happiness. In order to bring this happiness to your inner child, you will need a small crystal and a natural stone bracelet. I have created a few inner child bracelets in my "Magic Garden" spiritual jewelry series that serve the purpose of this practice, and I also sell the Cardinal Method Inner Child Kits as mentioned in Chapter 1. You can find them in the online store of my website www.ranovalife.com, or you can use *any* other stone bracelet and crystal for this practice.

Let your intuition guide you about which crystal to choose and which type of stones should be in your bracelet.

The small crystal you choose represents you as a child, and the stone bracelet represents a healthy boundary for your life and for the presence of your inner child in the world too. Remember, your inner child will always have a place in the world, but it cannot run the show of your adult life; otherwise, you will not grow.

The Practice

This healthy boundary has two purposes. First of all, it symbolizes not only a protection from any harm from the outside, but it also allows in only what is good and nurturing for you, kind of like cell walls that allow in nutrients and allow out garbage.

Second, and equally important, it kindly places your inner child in its rightful place within your psyche, instead of allowing it to take over areas that are not at all designed to be ruled by your inner child. Your adult life must be ruled by your higher self and not by any other aspect of your psyche. With the symbol of this healthy boundary (which is on the cover of this book for that purpose), your inner child will be respected in its rightful place and will respect the areas that are not meant for it to take over.

To start this exercise, lie down and close your eyes. Place a lavender eye pillow over them if you want. Lavender pillows are very soothing and help you get in a state of relaxation faster.

Put the small crystal over your heart or solar plexus (the solar plexus is on your stomach area) and then place the stone bracelet around the crystal, symbolically creating a circular healthy boundary around your inner child (represented by the crystal). You can find a picture of a "Magic Garden" stone bracelet around a crystal on the cover of this book.

Relax your whole body. Allow yourself to be in this state of bliss for a few minutes.

Think of yourself as a child between the ages of four and seven. This period of time is usually when a child is hurt and the subconscious mind decides to spend the rest of your life re-creating that wound in a useless effort to repair it.

As you think of yourself as a child, feel any emotion that may surface. Allow your emotions to communicate with you. This is very healing for your soul too, both individual and collective, because the Truth of some of the things that really bother you will come to light for emotional release.

After you have breathed in and out for a few moments, imagine your inner child being embraced by your mother and father. Visualize this scene and take as long as you need.

Take deep breaths. Next, you will allow your adult self to come into the visualization and imagine your parents sending your inner child to the arms of your adult self.

Feel how secure it is to be in the arms of your responsible adult self, and hear your adult self whisper: "*I see you. You have a place in my life. I will always take care of you. You are safe.*"

Take deep breaths and relax more and more. Allow your inner child to be in the arms of your adult self for as long as you need.

Keep breathing and relaxing. If you feel you need to sleep a little, do it.

When you feel like the process is complete, open your eyes slowly and smile.

Place the crystal and the bracelet on a bed of coarse sea salt and say a prayer of gratitude.

This simple practice not only heals your inner child, but it also gives you strength to embrace your adult life with all the best energies it has to give you.

7

STRENGTHENING A POSITIVE EGO WITH THE GRATITUDE FLOW

When you think about the problems in your life caused by your ego, observe your resistance. The flow of life is all about allowing the best energies to align with you. Whatever you resist in positive energy may be a controlling tendency caused by your ego.

Observe in which areas of your life your perfectionism and the invalidation of yourself and others take place. Observe also how your conscious mind invalidates emotions and spiritual practices.

The ego is a strong force in our psyche that allows us to move forward and make a difference in the world. Like the inner child, it has a sense of independence and personal power, but that should not override other fundamental aspects of life such as emotions, spirituality, and the higher self.

When the ego is out of balance, it disqualifies how you feel. It wants to be efficient and thinks feelings will take energy away from productivity and survival. This is a problem because when feelings are not validated, they become stagnant energy and may cause distortions on a subtle level and sometimes even on the physical level of your body.

In the perspective of Your Cardinal Connections, the best way to deal with, acknowledge, and dissolve resistance of the ego to true genuine feelings is to be grateful. Connect to the virtue of gratitude. This is why I developed the Gratitude Flow practice.

The ego may disqualify many feelings and emotions, but it does understand and respect gratitude. Gratitude is an antidote to the ego's dismissal and disqualification of feelings in general—both your own feelings and other people's feelings as well. Gratitude asks you to engage your conscious mind in acknowledging all your blessings with logical thinking and simultaneously with an open heart.

Gratitude is a feeling, and it is stronger than the ego. It brings peace and sobriety to your mind and literally gets you out of the "re-action to imperfections" trance.

It also helps to harmonize irrational emotions that attach you to past pain. It calms down the ego and puts it in its rightful place, which is to understand the world objectively so that it can serve the higher self. The higher self can then take charge of your life in peace and bring the best of your talents and love to the world.

When we connect to gratitude, the ego begins to acknowledge the value of every person, experience, and situation in our lives. We see the higher wisdom behind each experience and each relationship, as we thank life for all the blessings we have received and move forward.

The practice below will help bring in the Gratitude Flow and align your ego with your higher self. Hold a crystal you really love, and you can start.

The Gratitude Flow Practice
As said before, this practice not only helps to clear your energy, but it also calms the ego down and opens space for your feelings to be acknowledged so life can flow in its full potential.

This new energetic space enables you to strengthen Your Cardinal Connections as life becomes clearer and brighter, and as things seem to flow more abundantly and freely.

Your energetic space is who you are as an individual and as part of a collective soul—your family, the groups you belong to, and the world as a whole. With this practice, you will be cleaning and aligning your inner world and connecting yourself to the flow of life in which you meet the best people and find the best opportunities in life.

Unlike the inner child practice, which can be done daily and in less than twenty minutes, the Gratitude Flow has a more complex and mathematical structure. It is done in a rhythm of seven minutes, once a week, throughout seven weeks. This is the time it takes for the crystal energy to clear out the blockages of your ego and for you to be realigned with the power of your higher self.

The Seven-Week Meditation Process
For this self-healing process, the first thing you need to do is choose a single crystal to use during the practice. Try not to change crystals for each week's meditation for the sake of consistency and connection with a single crystal that represents your integration.

The crystal you will use can be any crystal that you already have with you, or you may purchase a new crystal for this practice, but make sure it is a crystal that you really love. The choice of the crystal is yours. Let your intuition guide you. There are no rules about colors, shapes, or sizes, though it is more comfortable to hold a crystal that fits in your hands and is not too rough.

Remember that the crystal you choose will guide you through the healing of seven aspects of your psyche that may be restricted by your ego and not allowing gratitude to flow.

The Practice

1. You will do a weekly awareness practice that lasts seven minutes (sometimes with affirmations, sometimes with visualizations, and sometimes in silence).
2. You will only do this practice for seven minutes once a week. Respect this rhythm because it took years of research and experience to develop this practice. This is literally a process that removes blockages imposed by your go and activates the power of your higher self.
3. Throughout the following six days, the energy will be healing the specific area of your life that you will have your focused on—the area of each weekly meditation, which corresponds to a layer of your psyche. On week 1 you will be clearing your relationship with God, on week 2, your relationship with your parents, on week 3 your relationship with your inner child, and so on. These layers of the psyche you will address must be done one at a time, once a week.
4. Each seven-minute practice will be done only once in a day of the week that you choose. The next practices should be done on the same day of the week of the subsequent week. It is important to be consistent with the day of the week. It does not matter which day you choose, as long as you stick to that day for the seven weeks. For example, if you choose to do your practice on Sunday, do it on the Sunday of the following week. Do not skip a week and wait for two weeks because you will break the rhythm of the healing.

5. Please be mindful of this seven-day interval between meditations. Do not start on Sunday and then decide to do the next one on a Friday or another day. For the sake of consistency, I also recommend you do not switch crystals for each meditation of the week and try to keep the same crystal for the 49 days.

6. After you have done the practice, the rest of the days before the next layer is addressed will probably bring you more awareness and flashes of moments and aspects of your life to be grateful for. You will notice those pop-ups coming up. Remember that crystals are very powerful in bringing information and promoting a flow of energy that unblocks resistance for the best potentials of life to flow.

7. Please respect the number seven. It is important for the ego to release resistance when it is following a rule of mathematical nature, even a simple one like that. The ego and the conscious mind tend to like the fact that you will be connected for seven minutes per meditation, one day a week, throughout seven weeks, because it is fairly logical and will cause less resistance.

8. Remember that silence is healing. Speaking to other people about your own healing may be nice, but your insights will be more powerful throughout the seven weeks if you can remain silent about your practice and just observe, feel, and release energetic blockages. You can talk to a close friend or a partner, but talking too much usually disrupts the healing process. Remember that silence is healing.

Below you will find the list of affirmations for each week of practice.

As said before, the wisdom of your heart will guide you in the choice of your crystal.

After the seven weeks are over, you can start a new process with a different crystal or with the same one, if you wish.

The Seven-Week Gratitude Flow Practice
Affirmations and Guidelines
As said before, dedicate seven minutes once a week to each practice. Set a timer before you start so you'll be connected to this exact amount of time.

Sit in a comfortable position. Do not lie down; be seated for this practice. You do not want to encourage your mind that you may sleep by lying down. Also, your chakras are better aligned in a vertical position.

Hold your crystal in your hands, preferably in Mandala Mudra. You have a picture of this hand position on the back cover of this book.

Repeat each affirmation when appropriate, because some weeks will be silent. Repeat the affirmations without stopping, exactly like a mantra, for the seven minutes. This means you will repeat the affirmation out loud continuously for seven minutes as you take deep breaths. Remember to say the affirmations out loud and to keep them in your mind throughout the process.

First Week: Honoring God: Affirmation

"Dear God, thank you for my life."

Repeat this affirmation calmly and continuously with the crystal in your hands in mandala for seven minutes.

Second Week: Honoring your Ancestors and Parents: Affirmation

"All my dear ancestors, thank you for my life."

"Dear Dad, thank you for my life."

"Dear Mom, thank you for my life."

Repeat these three affirmations calmly and continuously with the crystal in your hands in Mandala Mudra for seven minutes.

Third Week: Healing the Chakras: Visualization

No affirmations. You will just engage in silent visualization of a vertical energy flow coming through each one of the seven main chakras in the body (root, sacral, solar plexus, heart, throat, third eye, and crown).

You will imagine the flow of each chakra moving from top to bottom, from crown to root, as you breathe deeply and in silence.

Fourth Week: Healing the Inner Child: Affirmation

Visualize yourself as a child between the ages of four and seven and repeat the affirmation:

"My inner child, I see you. I love you."

Repeat this affirmation while visualizing yourself as a child, as if you were speaking to her or him, calmly and continuously, as you hold the crystal in your hands in Mandala Mudra for seven minutes.

Fifth Week: Healing All Your Relationships with Ho'oponopono: Affirmation

Repeat the affirmation for seven minutes in order to heal all your relationships with people, places, objects, events, and ideas. You may intentionally focus on a specific person or idea or object, or just allow them to pop up spontaneously in your mind. Repeat continuously:

"I love you, I'm sorry, please forgive me, thank you."

Ho'oponopono is a traditional Hawaiian prayer, and it is very powerful. Repeat the Ho'oponopono prayer calmly and continuously with the crystal in your hands in Mandala Mudra for seven minutes.

Sixth Week: Connecting to the Silent Observer: Silence
No affirmation. Be silent for seven minutes as you hold the crystal in your hands in Mandala Mudra. If you need to focus on something, focus on your third-eye chakra (between your eyebrows) by visualizing a light there or feeling its energy on your forehead.

Seventh Week: Connecting to Abundance: Affirmation

> "I am connected to the infinite flow of Love,
> freedom, and abundance in my life."

Repeat this affirmation calmly and continuously with the crystal in your hands in Mandala Mudra for seven minutes.

This seven-week process will help heal the excessive resistance of your ego to your feelings and to the expansion of your life with a flow of gratitude. You may repeat it as many times as you wish, and life will only get better the more you practice the Gratitude Flow.

Q&A

I have practiced all the suggestions published in this book for many years and have also observed clients and friends change their lives with these practices. I decided to bring some of the questions I was asked so they may clarify issues for you.

Do I need to clean the crystal after each meditation?
Not necessarily, only if you feel that you need to. The crystal will be charging positive energy in your life and discharging negative energy from it, but it does not need to be cleansed all the time. It's a proactive journey, and you may feel the crystal needs to accumulate energy from the previous meditation.

If your intuition tells you need to cleanse it, you can discharge the crystals with running water or lay it on dry salt beds if you feel it is appropriate. Remember to always say a prayer or a sacred mantra to your crystal after you clear it with salt or water.

Do I need to do anything special with the crystal between meditations, such as keeping it on me or nearby?
No, you do not. Place it on your altar or in a pouch and you will be good to go.

Can I use a mala bead or a bracelet, or should I choose a one-piece crystal?
You can use your mala or bracelet, but a single crystal is a better reminder of wholeness, oneness, and integration.

Can I be in a reclining position if I need to?
Yes, you can be in a reclining position if you are in physical pain or if you have physical limitations and sitting with a straight back is uncomfortable for you. However, it is best to be in yoga easy-pose or sitting on a chair with a straight back for this meditation.

Can I listen to soft music while doing the practice?

Yes, you can listen to soft music while doing the practice with affirmations and visualizations. From my own experience, I suggest you choose instrumentals or nature sounds because words and lyrics can be distracting.

Are there different types of Mandala Mudra? If so, which one should I use?

Yes, there are different types of Mandala Mudras, and the one I suggest you use is in the picture on the back of this book.

After the first meditation, I have noticed that it was easier to just appreciate life and people. I have also noticed abusive people, victims, bullies, and misery around me with more awareness. Does this have to do with the meditation?

Yes, it does. Your levels of awareness will rise and increase your perception of the outside world. This will increase with each week of the practice because you are expanding and strengthening your own healing energy.

Do we start perceiving more synchronicity and signs that guide us in directions and toward good decision-making?

Yes, you tend to start noticing good coincidences and synchronicity in events. You will also feel more clarity and general emotional well-being.

In the first week I felt a little calmer, and the affirmation popped into my head a few times during the day. It felt very comforting. In today's meditation I had some resistance to start the practice, but I kept going and warmed up to it. After the practice I was feeling grateful. Is each process different in each week?

Yes, each process is different in each week. Since you will be addressing different layers of the psyche, there may be more resistance in one or the other, and the energy may flow easily in other layers. You may have more resistance toward your parents, for example, than toward God, or more resistance to the silent observer than to the inner child. It depends a lot on how each person's ego is structured as a result of individual life experiences.

If I forget the meditation on one week, do I have start over from the first week? Or can I pick up where I left off? For example, if I do OK on the first three weeks and forget the fourth, can I do meditation #4 on the next week—which would technically be for the fifth meditation?

If that happens, I recommend you start over from the first week. With this practice, you are engaging in a continuous flow of gratitude. If you forget a week, that is where you find more resistance and probably where your ego needs healing the most—exactly where you have more resistance. Starting over may seem tedious, but it will actually strengthen your commitment and your responsibility for self, and it will bring you more discipline, persistence, and strength to help integrate your ego, your emotions, and your personal spiritual growth.

If I feel I need to switch crystals, can I do that?

It is best if you don't. This is typically another resistance mechanism that usually comes from your head and not from the heart. It is a minor sabotaging strategy when we try to complicate things instead of letting them flow in unity. Some people want to change their crystals and continue the practice with another one, but that weakens the energy. If this happens, pay attention to which layer of the psyche created the urge for interruption (which week it was) and be aware that you need more healing there.

If the crystal I was using is missing and I cannot find it anywhere, can I still do it with another crystal? Will that break the flow?

You can use another crystal if the one you were using before has disappeared, but I suggest you keep the same crystal throughout the whole process of seven weeks. If you lose the crystal, find another one and start over from the first week. The crystal symbolizes integration and unity. It is better to use another one from the first week and start all over again than to interrupt the process by changing crystals.

If I have physical symptoms—a cold, the flu, nausea, foggy head, etc.—does it have to do with the practice?
Physical symptoms are not caused by this practice. Crystal meditations are very subtle and act in the consciousness level in a sense of awareness. They do not cause anything and do not do anything to you. They allow information to surface to your consciousness. They help us solve our problems because they bring us more awareness and encourage responsibility for self. This practice was designed to help you understand your choices and what has led you to your present life situation. If you have physical symptoms, they were not caused by the practice.

Trust the fact that crystals help the healing process. They tune us into our hearts, our souls, and our awareness. They can never harm us, and they are not causal factors of physical symptoms. They are tools to remind us of our virtues and our love for self and others.

If I like the seven-week practice so much, can I start immediately on the following week with another crystal?
Yes, you absolutely can.

Can I do the practice lying down?
I suggest you sit down in easy and comfortable poses for the practice so your back is straight and aligned and all chakras are in vertical position. The body gets confused when we are lying down—it thinks we are sleeping, and we want to engage the conscious mind in the awareness of a Gratitude Flow. It is better to give the body accurate information in your posture so it knows you are awake and aware of what is going on.

If I am harsh with myself for missing a day of the practice and having to start over, what do I do?
Connect to the wisdom and kindness of your heart and remind yourself that no one is infallible or perfect, and remember that everything happens for a reason. If you are consciously making an effort to do this practice and doing your part, there is a deeper unconscious resistance that made you forget. Just knowing this may bring you more consciousness and awareness of which area of your life needs to be worked on.

This could also be a sign that you should do your practice with a different crystal. Think about this and see if it resonates.

Breaking resistance patterns is not always easy. It takes commitment and discipline. In this case, it requires an effort to integrate the conscious mind, the ego, and the heart into the Gratitude Flow, and start over with kindness and determination. Remind yourself that starting over will make you stronger.

APPENDIX 1

Cleaning, Discharging, and Charging Crystals

There are many ways to clean crystals. The most recommended one is to place them in a dry sea salt bowl and pour some dry sea salt crystals over them. Then send your breath to the crystals and you will be good to go.

Depending on the crystal you are using, you may put it under running water, but many crystals should not be wet (e.g., tourmaline, selenite, and kyanite). You may find recommendations to leave them in salt water or under the sun, but this is something I do not recommend. In more than twenty years of working with crystals, I have noticed salt water is corrosive, and sunlight often fades the colors of crystal, unless it is a white or clear piece. In my experience, I have noticed direct sunlight can be aggressive. Moonlight, on the other hand, is very nurturing to crystals.

In my experience, running water is fine as long as it does not take more than a few seconds, and sunlight is also OK as long as the crystal is exposed for no more than five minutes.

Singing bowls, Reiki, sound healing, sage smudging, moonlight, starlight, mantras, and prayers are also very effective.

Placing crystals in a bowl of dry sea salt crystals is usually the best way to cleanse them, followed by a breath on the crystal and/or a prayer or mantra.

Charging Crystals

Crystals get recharged with prayers, loving thoughts, and also by being placed for a few minutes on the earth. It can be on the earth of an indoor plant or the earth outside in a garden. Since crystals come from the earth, they get nurtured by Mother Nature.

The Crystal Flow

The flow of crystals, like life, is never obvious. This means they go wherever they need to go in their own timing. You never "belong" to a crystal, nor does a crystal (or crystal jewelry, for that matter) ever belong to you. You spend time together for a while, and then the flow of life will take them where they need to go. If you feel like you should give a crystal away or buy a crystal for someone, do it. That person needs to connect to that particular piece, and this is communicated to you by intuition.

APPENDIX 2

List of Recommended Crystals to Help Strengthen *Your Cardinal Connections*
The list below gives you some suggestions about the best crystals to have if you wish to strengthen *Your Cardinal Connections.*

Ancestral Healing (Earth Chakra)
Black tourmaline, smoky quartz, and clear quartz

Connection to the Earth, the Physical World, and the Present Moment (Earth Chakra)
Hematite

Protection from Ancestral Karma or Curses (Earth Chakra)
Andalusite

Connection and Ability to Take the Strength from Grandparents and Parents (Root Chakra)
Red jasper, red garnet, spessartite/spessartine garnet, red sapphire

Abundance, Pleasure, Allowing Life to Be Great (Sacral Chakra)
Carnelian, fire agate

Self Esteem, Confidence
Citrine, golden tiger eye

Emotional Healing
Green calcite, green quartz

Life Connection
Peridot

Self-Love, Self-Care, Unconditional Love, Compassion, Forgiveness
Rose quartz, rhodochrosite, rhodonite, morganite, pink calcite, danburite

Organizing Your Emotions
Green fluorite

Creativity, Healthy Communication, Authenticity
Chrysocholla, gem silica, turquoise, topaz, aquamarine

Intuition, Insight, Accuracy, Mental Clarity, Wisdom, Understanding, Faith
Lapiz lazuli, sodalite, blue sapphire, blue labradorite

Mental Cleansing, Releasing Belief Systems, Integrity
Lepidolite, tanzanite

Connection with God, Universal Life Force
Clear quartz, white apophilite, white selenite

Angelic Protection
Angelite, celestite, blue lace agate, blue kyanite, seraphinite

Ancestral Healing
Rubelite, ruby

Higher Hierarchy Protection
Diamonds

EPILOGUE

I am very grateful you have reached the end of this book. I truly hope it has helped you in some way.

You will feel that *Your Cardinal Connections* are very powerful. They help you eliminate negativity and blockages from your life, and you can align yourself with joyful, truthful, loving experiences.

My best wishes to you in this journey. I hope to see you again on my YouTube channel, on my website, and through my other books in the future as well!

With all my love and gratitude,

Paola

REFERENCES

The Pathwork of Self-Transformation, Eva Pierrakos

Creating Union: The Essence of Intimate Relationship, Eva Pierrakos and Judy Sally

Zero Limits: The Secret Hawaiian System for Wealth, Health, Peace and More, Joe Vitale and Ihaleakala Hew Len

Make Every Man Want You: How to Be So Irresistible You'll Barely Keep from Dating Yourself, Marie Forleo

The Science and Philosophy of BodyTalk—Healthcare Designed by Your Body, John Veltheim

Family Constellations. Basic Principles and Procedures, Jakob Robert Schneider

Quiet: The Power of Introverts in a World that Can't Stop Talking, Susan Cain

Alchemy of Love Relationships, Joseph Michael Levry (Gurunam)

Crystals, Minerals and Stones, Margaret Lembo

The Crystal Bible 1, Judy Hall

The Crystal Bible 2, Judy Hall

The Crystal Bible 3, Judy Hall

The Crystal Experience, Judy Hall

Love is in the Earth, A Kaleidoscope of Crystals - The Reference Book Describing the Metaphysical Properties of the Mineral Kingdom, Melody (Author), Julianne Guilbault (Illustrator)

YOUR CARDINAL CONNECTIONS JOURNAL:
NOTES TO SELF

_____
_____
_____
_____
_____
_____
_____
_____
_____
_____
_____
_____
_____
_____
_____
_____
_____
_____
_____
_____
_____
_____
_____
_____
_____
_____
_____

43893637R00078

Made in the USA
San Bernardino, CA
31 December 2016